One Hundred and Fifty Years of Tragedy: Nietzsche, Art, Philosophy

Edited by Paris Lettau and Vincent Lê

Index Press

One Hundred and Fifty Years of Tragedy: Nietzsche, Art, Philosophy

First published in Australia in 2025 by Index Press
Printed in Australia

Index Press
The Nicholas Building
Suite 703, 37 Swanston Street
Naarm / Melbourne VIC 3000
Australia

index-press.com

Index Press acknowledges and pays respect to the elders of the Kulin Nations as the owners of the lands and waters on which we live and work. Aboriginal sovereignty was never ceded.

Index Press Inc. is an incorporated association registered in Victoria, Australia.

Edited by Paris Lettau and Vincent Lê
Proofreading by Sam Cooney and Loqui Paatsch
Design by Alexandra Margetic

ISBN 978-0-64862-971-9

A catalogue record for this book is available from the National Library of Australia.

Contents

Acknowledgements

This book originated from a seminar hosted by the Melbourne School of Continental Philosophy (MSCP) at the University of Melbourne. We wish to thank the MSCP and the School of Culture and Communication in the Faculty of Arts at the University of Melbourne for generously supporting both the seminar and this publication. We extend our sincere gratitude to all contributors for their thoughtful chapters and insightful discussions. Finally, we are grateful to our peer reviewers and early readers for their valuable feedback.

List of Abbreviations

Where abbreviations are utilised, Nietzsche's works are cited in the following format: title abbreviation, book number, essay number, section name, aphorism number, and page number. Authors may refer in footnotes to a specific edition if utilised.

Collected Works

KSA	*Friedrich Nietzsche: Sämtliche Werke: Kritische Studienausgabe*
WP	*The Will to Power*

Individual Works

AC	*The Anti-Christ*
ASC	*Attempt at Self-Criticism*
BGE	*Beyond Good and Evil: Prelude to a Philosophy of the Future*
BT	*The Birth of Tragedy: or Hellenism and Pessimism*
BTT	*The Birth of Tragic Thought*
CW	*The Case of Wagner: A Musician's Problem*
D	*Daybreak*
DD	*The Dithyrambs of Dionysus*
DS	*David Strauss, the Confessor and Writer*
DW	*The Dionysian World-View*
EH	*Ecce Homo: How One Becomes What One Is*
FE	*The Future of our Educational Institutions*
GDG	*Der Gottesdienst der Griechen*
GG	*Die Geburt des tragischen Gedankens*
GGL	*Geschichte Griechische Literatur 1–3*
GM	*The Genealogy of Morals: A Polemic*
GMD	*Griechische Musik Drama*
GS	*The Gay Science*
HC	*Homer's Contest*
HH	*Human, All Too Human*
HL	*On the Use and Abuse of History for Life*
MM	*Mixed Opinions and Maxims*
NCW	*Nietzsche contra Wagner*
PPP	*The Pre-Platonic Philosophers*
PTG	*Philosophy in the Tragic Age of the Greeks*
SE	*Schopenhauer as Educator*
SGT	*Socrates and Greek Tragedy*
ST	*Socrates and Tragedy*
TI	*Twilight of the Idols, or How to Philosophize with a Hammer*
TL	*On Truth and Lying in a Non-moral Sense*
UO	*Unfashionable Observations*
WB	*Richard Wagner in Bayreuth*
WPh	*We Philologens*
WS	*The Wanderer and his Shadow*
Z	*Thus Spoke Zarathustra: A Book for All and None*

Introduction: Nietzschean Vibe Shifts

Paris Lettau and Vincent Lê

Introduction

Nietzsche's first book, *The Birth of Tragedy Out of the Spirit of Music*, was a commercial failure, selling only a few hundred copies when first published in January 1872. And yet, more than 150 years later, its impact is incalculable. In this audacious debut, published when he was just twenty-seven years old, Nietzsche traces the evolution of tragic art as a struggle between two primal forces: the measured harmony of Apollo and the intoxicating chaos of Dionysus. He sees in Greek tragedy an unflinching affirmation of life's suffering—an aesthetic and existential embrace that rationalism would later seek to suppress. He admires the Greek classicists and modern romantics alike for their capacity to confront and even revel in art's depiction of humanity's agonies, afflicted by nature and the gods. Against them, he sets the rationalist tradition that, in his view, found its most fateful expression in Socrates, whose banishment of the tragic poets from his ideal republic marked a turning point in Western thought. Or so goes the usual summary.

Though the book was hardly read when first published, Nietzsche's prediction that he would be "born posthumously" was vindicated.[1] Since the early twentieth century, his voice has echoed across generations. Spread so widely, no wonder few thinkers have been more contested, nor more radically divided between champions and critics. As Walter Kaufmann observed, "In Nietzsche's case there is not even basic agreement about what he stood for: His admirers are as much at odds about this as his critics."[2] And so it remains. Each year, university presses churn out new studies on Nietzsche. Yet unlike most philosophers, Nietzsche's influence extends far beyond the ivory tower, with his ideas continually resurfacing in ideological battles and viral cultural moments. Providing a new cosmology that echoes the cruel fate of a Darwinian humanity, his ideas also penetrated deeply, shaping the psyche of the post-Enlightenment age in which we still live. In this, he is less a philosopher than a prophet, whose radical anti-Christian spirit continues to inflame with near-religious intensity.

Consider contrasting contemporary ideologues that embrace his legacy.

On one side, Jordan Peterson, pseudonymous far-right internet personality Bronze Age Pervert ("BAP"), and alt-right and neoreactionary intellectual circles seize upon Nietzsche's critique of modernity—his denunciation of democracy, feminism, and herd morality—to champion a return to the supposed nobility and virility of the ancient Greeks. For BAP, Nietzsche's philosophy is a call to arms against what he sees as the unmanly, degenerate forces of the contemporary world. "Nietzsche said manliness is the first requirement of the philosopher," he proclaims, "but there's no one farther from the philosopher than the unmanly nerd, and there's no enemy more implacable of the human race and of the genius of the species, than just this nerd and everything he represents."[3]

Yet, the very "nerds" whom BAP scorns—those in the transhumanist and effective accelerationist movements—draw inspiration from Nietzsche in an entirely different register. For them, his vision of a coming Übermensch that would surpass humanity prefigures the radical possibilities of biotechnology and artificial intelligence, which promise to shatter the limits of our all-too-human condition. In his 2023 "Techno-Optimist Manifesto," Marc Andreessen, co-creator of the first web browser Netscape Navigator, identifies Nietzsche's "last man" as the ultimate adversary, and exhorts his readers: "If you read the work" of Nietzsche, "you too will become a Techno-Optimist."[4]

Unholy alliances also surround Nietzsche's name today. In a 2024 interview with Andreessen following Donald Trump's re-election, popular podcaster Joe Rogan described Dick Cheney's endorsement of Kamala Harris as the "Nietzschean vibe shift." When an alliance between an evangelical Republican war hawk and "woke" Democrat is framed in Nietzschean terms, we know a paradigm has taken hold.

Can we really comprehend it, judge its worthiness, its use, as our history piles up around us and our future rings ever more loudly in our ears? Not while we are still in it, unable to discern its horizon. The strategy we have therefore adopted in this book is to follow Nietzsche's musings with a genealogy of those who have succumbed to his sermons.

Why a genealogy? Because no consensus has ever been reached on what "Nietzsche" means. He has been championed as a prophet of aristocratic radicalism, a proto-fascist, a postmodern relativist, a transhumanist, an anarchist, an existentialist, and a reactionary. He has been invoked in Silicon Valley boardrooms and underground meme forums by radical individualists and collectivist revolutionaries alike. From Camille Paglia's Nietzschean feminism to Jordan Peterson's conservative Nietzsche, from the Dionysian aesthetics of avant-garde art to the accelerationist fantasies of AI utopians, the name "Nietzsche" now signifies everything—and nothing—at once. In this situation, where nothing is defined, all we have are the blurred outlines of filiations—a tangled inheritance of missed meanings and misinterpretations along which we can only stumble.

Ours is a mere sketch. A full genealogy would trek through so many more wastelands, tracing the shifting and contradictory ways Nietzsche's thought has been received, appropriated, and reinvented. And yet we begin where genealogies always begin—now, at the end of an inheritance, as if we are its destiny.

The first chapter situates Nietzsche's reception in its most contested terrain—his afterlife in political and philosophical interpretation. In "The Death of Nietzsche," Caitlyn Lesiuk examines the radically divergent ways in which Nietzsche has been read, appropriated, and manipulated to support contradictory ideological ends. She traces how Nietzsche's works have been selectively interpreted—through a process akin to "philosophizing with scissors," as Peter Sloterdijk describes it—by figures across the political spectrum, from fascist propagandists to Marxist revolutionaries, from existentialists to postmodern theorists. Lesiuk draws out the historical and methodological implications of this fragmented reception, questioning whether Nietzsche's philosophy can ever be decisively situated within a coherent political framework. She challenges the impulse to reconstruct Nietzsche's "true" meaning through biography, claiming his works resist closure and demand a mode of reading more like Nietzsche's own aesthetic listener in *The Birth of Tragedy*. Lesiuk asks whether Nietzsche's reception history reveals not the instability of his thought, but the inescapable contradictions at the heart of philosophical interpretation itself.

Chapter two moves back to the late twentieth century, tracing Nietzsche's legacy in postmodern philosophy. In "The Forced Choice of Post-Modernism: Alenka Zupančič's Nietzsche," Rex Butler claims Nietzsche's philosophy aimed to "break the world in two," shaping a generation of French thinkers—including Derrida, Deleuze, Lyotard, and Baudrillard—who were especially influential in intellectual circles during the 1980s. Butler argues that this postmodern Nietzscheanism can only exist as a tradition of singularities, where each philosopher enacts Nietzsche's own logic of doubling, producing a new Nietzsche by fragmenting him. Butler calls on Slovenian philosopher Alenka Zupančič, and Nietzsche's image of the paradoxical "shortest shadow," visible at midday—a moment when no shadow should exist—interpreting it as the very split that allows opposition itself to be perceptible. Butler situates this insight within modern art by engaging with Zupančič's comparison of Nietzsche's shadow to Kazimir Malevich's *Black Square* (1915) and *Suprematist Composition: White on White* (1918), arguing that Nietzsche's thought inaugurates a radical break that both constructs and destabilises the conceptual foundations of postmodernism.

The third chapter moves into the early twentieth century, examining Nietzsche's reception in the Australian art world. In "Dionysos in the Antipodes: Nietzsche, Norman and Jack Lindsay, Bernard Smith," Ian McLean explores how Nietzsche's thought shaped the work of Norman Lindsay, a prolific Australian artist and self-declared Nietzschean, and his son Jack Lindsay, whose *Dionysos: Nietzsche contra Nietzsche* (1928) sought to extend his father's vision into a more systematic engagement with Nietzschean ideas. McLean discusses the impact of Nietzsche on their thinking, including the paradoxical relations of Nietzsche's views on sexuality and gender in Lindsay's signature depictions of libidinous women. He also investigates how this father–son duo came to the attention of Australia's foremost art historian Bernard Smith. McLean argues that while Smith found inspiration in Jack Lindsay's writings, which attempted to reconcile Nietzsche's radicalism with a leftist, historicist perspective on art and culture, he never arrived at a resolved position on Nietzsche and Lindsay's place in the story of Australian art. Smith's ambivalence ranged from viewing the father–son duo as exemplifying everything wrong with twentieth-century modernism, to Lindsay being among the most radical of Australian artists. While Smith dismissed Nietzsche as a dangerous elitist, Nietzsche's ideas also infiltrated Smith's thinking. This contested reception, McLean concludes, echoes in Smith's later writing as he sought to come to terms with Indigenous art and the postcolonial shifts that unsettled his canonical history of Australian art.

Following Nietzsche's early reflections on art and tragedy, "Taking Flight from Oneself: Nietzsche on the Poets, Baudelaire, and the Little Parisian Decadents" sees Keith Ansell-Pearson address Nietzsche's evolving engagement with poetry and decadence in the late nineteenth century. Ansell-Pearson argues that Nietzsche's middle period (1878–82) marks a decisive shift away from the aesthetic metaphysics of *The Birth of Tragedy*, as the philosopher turns a more critical eye to art and poetry, reproaching poets for their melancholic introspection and tendency to dwell on the past rather than point toward the future. However, as Ansell-Pearson highlights, Nietzsche also identifies a more affirmative poetic vision in figures like Adalbert Stifter, whose portrayal of "beautiful human beings" aligns with Nietzsche's vision of an art that cultivates higher forms of life. In his later writings (1883–88), Nietzsche sharpens his critique of decadence, particularly in relation to French literature, associating Baudelaire with Wagnerian nihilism and the exhaustion of modernity. Ansell-Pearson complicates this reading by drawing on Walter Benjamin's interpretation of Baudelaire, which presents the poet not as a decadent pessimist but as a "brooder" whose work resists the nihilistic resignation Nietzsche abhors. Ansell-Pearson argues that Nietzsche's attitude toward poetry is deeply ambivalent: while he sees it as capable of envisioning higher forms of life, he also critiques its descent into decadence, particularly when it becomes an expression of cultural exhaustion rather than creative renewal.

The fifth chapter shifts focus to Nietzsche's early academic period and philological background. In "We Have Ways of

Making You Talk: Parsing Nietzsche's Philology," Jason Barker and Justin Clemens turn to Nietzsche's fraught relationship with philology, the discipline in which he was trained that he both practised and repudiated. They argue that Nietzsche's engagement with language, education, and interpretation cannot be separated from his philological formation, even as he sought to transcend it. The chapter looks to Nietzsche's academic career, his critique of the German educational system, and his later reflections on philology as an art of disruption rather than mere textual restoration. Drawing on examples from *The Birth of Tragedy* and *On the Future of Our Educational Institutions* (1872) to *Daybreak* (1881), Barker and Clemens situate Nietzsche's philological method within broader debates about knowledge, authority, and the limits of interpretation. They trace how Nietzsche's approach to language—wavering between precision and play, discipline and excess—foreshadows many of the concerns of twentieth-century philosophy, from deconstruction to genealogical critique.

The book's final chapter takes us back to the beginning—with the first sentence of the first book by our self-claimed uber-ancestor. In "Nietzsche's Birth of Tragedy: A Philosophy of Duality, Conflict, and Relationality," Vanessa Lemm undertakes a close reading of this foundational sentence, in which Nietzsche declares that the "continuous development of art is bound up with the duality of the Apollonian and the Dionysian in much the same way as reproduction depends on the duality of the sexes in a state of perpetual conflict, interrupted only occasionally by periods of reconciliation." Lemm argues that this opening statement establishes a guiding thread for Nietzsche's whole philosophy—a philosophy of twoness and agonistic struggle.

Against interpretations that treat Apollo and Dionysus as separate and opposing figures, Lemm claims that it is their entanglement that is essential: their creative tension does not resolve into unity but remains an irreducible force of discord that drives both life and art. She situates Nietzsche's concept of *Generation* (reproduction) within the biological and philosophical discourses of his time, showing how he aligns artistic creation with natural reproduction. Moving through

Nietzsche's engagements with the Pre-Socratics, Greek tragedy, and his later reflections on *Kampf* (struggle) and *Versöhnung* (reconciliation), Lemm reveals a thinker whose fundamental gesture is the affirmation of conflict as the very condition of creativity and becoming.

And so *One Hundred and Fifty Years of Tragedy* concludes where it began: with the seemingly irreconcilable struggle between conflicting perspectives. Having located conflict at the very heart of Nietzsche's thought—ever since his first book's opening lines—we can glimpse why his legacy was destined to become so highly contested and fought over, and why it continues to break our world in two.

1 Friedrich Nietzsche, "The Anti-Christ: A Curse on Christianity," in *The Anti-Christ, Ecce Homo, Twilight of the Idols, and Other Writings*, eds. Aaron Ridley and Judith Norman, trans. Judith Norman (Cambridge University Press, 2005), 3.

2 Walter Kaufmann, *Nietzsche: Philosopher, Psychologist, Antichrist* (Princeton University Press, 1974), 3.

3 Bronze Age Pervert, *Bronze Age Mindset: An Exhortation* (independently published, 2018), eBook.

4 Marc Andreessen, "The Techno-Optimist Manifesto," *Andreessen Horowitz*, October 16, 2023, accessed December 13, 2024, https://a16z.com/the-techno-optimist-manifesto/.

The Death of Nietzsche

Caitlyn Lesiuk

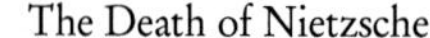
The Death of Nietzsche

The Repatriation General Hospital Chapel in suburban Adelaide, Australia, has a curious feature: the pews are bifid, so Roman Catholics can face the western wall of the church and Protestant or Church of England worshippers face to the east. This design was inspired by the local trams, "which could reverse the direction of their seating, rather than use a turntable for the carriages."[1] Constructed in 1942, along with a military hospital to service World War II veterans, it's an apt architectural reconstruction of how readers enter into critical engagement with Friedrich Nietzsche, especially given speculations that he laid a foundation for this conflict. The maxim *Pro captu lectoris, habent sua fata libelli,* which translates as "according to the capabilities of the reader, books have their destiny," has perhaps never been truer than in the case of his oeuvre. The political destinies of his works are as varied as they are contradictory. As Kurt Tucholsky puts it, "Who cannot make demands on him? Tell me what you need and I will find you a Nietzsche quotation for it . . . For Germany and against Germany; for peace and against peace; for literature and against literature."[2] It simply seems to be a matter of how you orient your pew. The required symbolism and even fellow parishioners will be there either way, but you must share the house of God with the opposing faith.

The way Nietzsche's readers relate to him is not unlike the way one might relate to a religious figure. The English translation of the title of Peter Sloterdijk's essay *Über die Verbesserung der guten Nachricht: Nietzsches fünftes "Evangelium"* as *Nietzsche Apostle* aptly reflects this. Sloterdijk likens readers of Nietzsche, especially academic ones, to Thomas Jefferson and Leo Tolstoy, who both offered creative syntheses of the canonical gospels. The more literal translation of the German title of his essay is something like *On the Improvement of the Good News,* the "good news" being the coming of Christ and the Kingdom of God as told in the Gospels. Sloterdijk describes how during Jefferson's first presidential term from 1801 to 1805, he began working on his own version of the New Testament. His first attempt was constructed from clippings taken from two King James editions. He extracted the statements of Jesus and pasted them into a forty-six-page scrapbook. The second, more comprehensive attempt, drew on versions of the Bible in several languages, including English, French, Greek, and Latin. The text was presented in a red, leather-bound book, with two columns. It told the story of Jesus with all miracles removed. Jefferson never intended this to be published—it was for his personal reference. This final version of the work completed in 1820 was titled *The Life and Morals of Jesus of Nazareth.*

This method of reading, which Sloterdijk calls "philosiphiz[ing] with scissors," serves to recreate texts based on the particular concerns of the reader.[3] For instance, Jefferson's Bible reconfigures Christ's story to suit certain ideas of "American glory," and opts for rationalism by removing anything seen to be supernatural.[4] Tolstoy's Bible is oriented toward reconciling "evangelism" with the "Enlightenment" for the new Russia.[5] We see similar manipulations of Nietzsche's works to support vastly different political and philosophical ends. What emerges from this historical tendency to read Nietzsche with scissors are many, seemingly contradictory versions of the thinker.

At least this cut-and-paste approach to the New Testament is part of an established hermeneutics in the Abrahamic religions. In fact, it is exactly how most of these religious texts were composed in a written form. Historically, through a necessity inspired by political unrest which demands the consecration of religious texts to preserve communities of faith, sacred texts have been subject to a process of contingent selection and redaction. For instance, the New Testament includes the canonical gospels of Matthew, Mark, Luke, and John but excludes an extensive number of apocrypha which were considered scripture by early Christians. There is also context for commentaries being raised to comparable status as the texts they treat. Although there are differences, the Talmud and Torah in Judaism are both considered crucial—the commentarial tradition in Judaism is a central component of the institutionalised faith. In Islam, the Hadith, which details the life of Mohammad, is also important, and there are different versions of this in different denominations.

However, this is *not* the way readers of philosophy have typically been taught to approach texts. One can't help but wonder: what is the precedent for responding to Nietzsche's works in this way? Biographer Sue Prideaux suggests that it is precisely because the notes Nietzsche left behind (the *Nachlass*) have been given the "status of Holy Writ" that various philosophers, biographers, and editors feel it appropriate to "cut and paste the dislocated fragments and reassemble them to convey their own ideas."[6] Behind this cut-up approach is a desire to understand a work by understanding its author, to make a case for the real *intention* behind the work. There is a strong tendency, contra Roland Barthes and the "death of the author," to turn to Nietzsche's unpublished notebooks and letters to divine his real meaning. Many Nietzsche scholars argue for the validity of their interpretation based on it being closest to what Nietzsche *really thought* about certain topics.

It is difficult to separate Nietzsche's works from the man Nietzsche. This is not least because of the strength and endearing nature of the voice that comes through in his texts, and the way he himself describes his works. Indeed, Nietzsche's publisher wanted to maintain a certain "momentum" by publishing an untimely meditation every nine months.[7] This is the same amount of time it takes for a human child to grow inside the womb, and we have a strong sense of Nietzsche's texts as his children. In a letter to Ewin Rhode in 1870, Nietzsche exclaimed that "scholarship, art, and philosophy are growing together inside me to such an extent that one day I'm bound to give birth to centaurs." He described *The Birth of Tragedy*, published two years later, to his sister Elisabeth as precisely such a "centaur." Not only Nietzsche's books, but also his readers, can be seen as his progeny. Joanne Faulkner argues that Nietzsche's readers form a parent–child relationship to his authorial voice, which accounts for why his works are "so abiding and formative" for so many.[8] Styles of reading focussing on Nietzsche's biography are also inspired by the constant sense of contradiction within Nietzsche's works at which we have already hinted. It is evident across Nietzsche's oeuvre that philosophers who present systematised programmes of thought are anathema to him, and it's hardly surprising that we find a lack of systematisation in his own work. Nietzsche revels in contradiction—and it is natural that we avoid preserving the difficult reality of his inconsistency.

Political Destinies: Nietzsche Between the Left and the Right

Firstly, what is the general sense of disorientation in Nietzsche scholarship regarding political readings of his oeuvre? Interpretations of Nietzsche have oscillated between the far left and the far right. At one extreme of these political poles is a relationship between Nietzsche and the Nazi regime. This legacy is interesting when one considers that Nietzsche passed away twenty years before the formation of the Nazi Party. Along with copies of the New Testament, "one hundred and fifty thousand copies of *Zarathustra* were printed in a special pocket edition for German soldiers in the First World War, to be taken into battle."[9]

Nietzsche's works have formed the raw material for a long line of cut-up artists, beginning with his sister Elisabeth and her right-wing preferences. During Nietzsche's decline into madness and after his death, Elisabeth had control of his literary estate, and compiled the *Nachlass* from a vast archive of unpublished notes, including whatever letters and drafts she could convince his friends and correspondents to return to her. We know that Nietzsche was very deliberate about what he published, and much of what later appeared in the posthumous publication *The Will to Power*, which is the text most associated with fascist sympathies, was not written for public consumption.[10]

Even more radical than Elisabeth was Alfred Bäumler's approach to the archive. Elisabeth at least sought to add to Nietzsche's published canon while continuing to circulate the existing works in the public domain. However, Bäumler, who according to Prideaux is "most responsible for establishing the link between Nietzsche and Hitler," sought to revise, if not completely redact the sentiment of *all* of Nietzsche's published works in his reconstruction of the Nietzsche-gospel.[11] Bäumler, along with Martin Heidegger, suggested that Nietzsche's "real philosophy" was in the *Nachlass*, and that, in the light of reading through the archive, any of his published works "hardly counted."[12] Despite the manipulation of Nietzsche's oeuvre to emphasise these aspects of his work, there is undeniably ammunition for the fascist thinker among both his published and unpublished writings. As methodically documented in Domenico Losurdo's *Aristocratic Rebel*, this takes the form of isolated anti-Semitic quotes, as well as certain interpretations of the eternal return and the will to power. It can also be identified in Nietzsche's broader methodological approach. As György Lukács argues in *The Destruction of Reason*, Nietzsche's anti-rationalist tendencies can be seen to lead to socially problematic conclusions. In questioning the value of all values, Nietzsche not only overturns the foundation of traditional morality but also clears the ground for new, potentially problematic schemas.

However, there is just as strong a connection between Nietzsche's thought and left-wing movements. Despite Geoff Waite's claim that Nietzsche is the "ultimate adversary" of communism, there have been many leftist appropriations of Nietzsche's thought.[13] In Nietzsche's day, a rich widow, Rosalie Nielson, attempted to get publishing rights for Nietzsche's books, eventually buying out Nietzsche and Richard Wagner's publisher to secure them. She had strong connections with the Marxist International, which at the time had identified Nietzsche "as politically one of their own."[14] And at the height of Nietzsche's popularity with the Nazi regime, Henri Lefebvre in 1939 wrote a book titled *Nietzsche* that interpreted his work as a useful resource for Marxism. Indeed, unlike another widely available work written by Lefebvre in the same year, *Nietzsche* was not republished until sixty years later, and most first editions were destroyed. This is precisely because it was "proscribed and burned" by Germans occupying France, for directly—and not unskillfully—countering the fascist reading.[15]

This split in interpretation persists in more recent scholarship, and some might say that it has even re-emerged in full force in the last ten years. With the English translation of Losurdo's *Aristocratic Rebel,* Harrison Fluss identifies a new "wave" of Nietzsche criticism, outlining his influence on the far right. The contention here is that Nietzsche's comments on subjects such as race and slavery are not extrinsic to his contribution to thought. Against a prevalent tendency to de-emphasise these aspects of his work, philosophers must include—if not *rewrite*—them into the history of Nietzsche scholarship. Losurdo is critical of the way that Nietzsche has been adopted by leftists, particularly, but not exclusively, in the Italian context. Indeed, while there is much in Nietzsche which questions the political status quo and encourages the reader to question cultural norms and values, Losurdo draws our eye back to the aristocratic character of his political imperative. Methodologically, Losurdo proceeds by rewriting Nietzsche's claims into the historical context in which he was composing, whether that be the general ideological and political situation, or the conditions around certain debates, for instance between "classical antiquity and Christianity."[16] He suggests that to understand Nietzsche's contribution to thought, we need to make the "untimely" author timely again. Scholars also look at the context of Nietzsche's claims on a micro-level. For example, one recent book on Nietzsche meticulously recreates where he placed a single, double, or triple underline in his notes, or made other markings such as drawing boxes around certain phrases.[17]

There are myriad political responses to Nietzsche beyond the Marxist and Nazi uptake. Fluss, following Losurdo, also cautions against readings which claim Nietzsche for liberalism. For instance, Jennifer Ratner-Rosenhagen suggests that Nietzsche's writings are productive for establishing identity in a post-Christian and post-moral world.[18] While she acknowledges the fundamental "indeterminacy" underlying Nietzsche's philosophy, she emphasises how his thought lends itself to a certain "pluralism" reconcilable with American democratic politics. There's also potential for the destructive or emancipatory political revolutionary latent in Nietzsche. Jürgen Habermas identifies the former in his analysis, suggesting that Nietzsche's proposed methods of overturning modernity would lead to social disintegration if adopted wholesale. Some argue it is a mistake to politicise him altogether, and such readings are generally accused of glossing over the potentially problematic elements of his work. This tradition, which Losurdo explicitly pits his account against, includes figures like Gianni Vattimo, Giorgio Colli, Michel Foucault, Gilles Deleuze, Walter Kaufmann, and Georges Bataille.[19] Losurdo groups these thinkers together under the accusation that they proclaim the innocence of Nietzsche, whether implicitly or explicitly.

The common denominator between these various streams of interpreting Nietzsche is the accusation that the opposing side is simply "cherry-picking" from Nietzsche's work. The reason we find such disparate readings and dissent in the scholarship is precisely a result of reading Nietzsche "with scissors," as Sloterdijk aptly puts it. Losurdo suggests philosophers become swept up in what he terms a "hermeneutics of innocence," pointing to Nietzsche's sister Elisabeth's influence on the framing of his texts (as we have admittedly done here), or in the act of translation, by choosing less shocking words when it comes to inflammatory terms like "breeding."[20] However, Losurdo argues, if we take a historical approach, Nietzsche appears unarguably among those who propagated the "anti-democratic movement" that eventuates in fascism.[21]

From the other side, we have the accusation that the elements indicating potentially problematic aspects of Nietzsche's work are over-emphasised, at the cost of looking past the philosophical import of his work entirely. Sloterdijk calls fascist readers of Nietzsche "boorish" in their handling of the nuances of his writing, invoking Thomas Mann, who claims that whoever reads Nietzsche "literally" by honing in on "content and semantic reduction" is "lost."[22] Or, as Foucault suggests, it's a matter of *how the text works* over *what the text means*, and we are mistaken to focus on the problem of "correct" or "incorrect" interpretations. He writes, "the only valid tribute to thought such as Nietzsche's is . . . to use it, to deform it, to make it groan and protest. And if commentators then say that I am being faithful or unfaithful, that is of absolutely no interest."[23] Or, particularly annoying to Losurdo is Colli's claim that we should read Nietzsche in the way we might listen to music. Compiling a one-for-one bifurcation of quotations and examples that contradict and support different characterisations of Nietzsche yields little. What is missing from each of these interpretations is Nietzsche's oeuvre taken as a contradictory whole, maintaining, rather than omitting, what supports the opposing viewpoint to a given critic.

The very possibility of sensibly drawing a politics from Nietzsche remains an open question, given the fundamental indeterminacy of his texts. The vastly different political elaborations on Nietzsche summarised here are not without grounds. What's more, the extent to which Nietzsche intended a political programme to be inscribed in his texts is debatable. For instance, *The Birth of Tragedy* achieves the "untimely" style of much of Nietzsche's writing by harking back to the Greeks rather than dwelling on the particularity of the politics of the day. However, he does indeed refer to the Franco-Prussian war, and it's clear that his critique of modernism is designed to transform the Germany not only of the future, but also of the present. That said, Nietzsche had an unmistakable distaste for politics. Prideaux notes that he was disturbed by Nielson buying out the publishing rights to his texts, partially because of the association with Marxism. We once again find ample support for conflicting interpretations.

Nietzsche offers some comments on the style of reading that emerges in academic and political responses to his texts, again playing the prophetic figure. For instance, regarding the opposing and problematic characterisations of his work, he says at one point, "I am frightened . . . of how my texts will be used": he notes that they have the potential to be both a "disaster" and a "blessing."[24] In *Human, All Too Human*, Nietzsche writes: "The worst readers are those who behave like plundering troops: they take away a few things they can use, dirty and confound the remainder, and revile the whole."[25] In *Ecce Homo*, he elaborates on this mode of reading, and critiques the figure of the scholar, in particular the philologist, who stops being able to think because he can only "trundle" books and react to what he finds therein, affirming or denying their contents. Nietzsche also anticipates his writings being misunderstood because their time and ideal readers had not yet come.[26] Indeed, he claims, "whoever believed he had understood something of me had dressed up something out of me after his own image."[27] But as Sloterdijk claims, despite all this, Nietzsche couldn't have guessed at the extent to which, "from the riff-raff he repelled, his most tenacious clientele [would] emerge."[28] If we think of the name Nietzsche as a kind of "designer," and his brand as "destiny," Sloterdijk argues he should have had better "copy protection" built in. We might think here of Alfred Hitchcock, who notoriously only shot enough footage for his films to be edited into the precise arrangement he intended.

Nietzsche confronts philosophers with a question proper to literary criticism: How do we read a text? The merits of the approaches we have summarised must be evaluated, especially regarding how much we should rely on biographical detail or look to the figure of the author in navigating challenging bodies of work. As we have seen, one of the consequences of using these factors to curate Nietzsche's output has been a general sense of dissent.

Socrates, whom Nietzsche loathed, addresses this question implicitly in the *Apology*. In *The Birth of Tragedy,* Nietzsche attributes the deterioration of the tragic spirit of art in the Hellenic tradition to a prioritisation of reason that can be traced back to the Platonic dialogues. Yet, despite Nietzsche's distaste for Socrates, there is something to be gleaned from the *Apology* when it comes to his interpreters. After being named by an oracle as the wisest of all men, Socrates describes his journey to seek out someone wiser than himself to refute the claim. He begins by questioning a public intellectual, and then the politicians, but finds them to be disillusioned. Socrates's wisdom is precisely in *knowing* that he knows nothing. It is in this respect that he is a measure wiser than those who think they *do* possess knowledge but cannot defend their claims under questioning. Socrates then turns his attention to the poets, asking them about the meaning of the great works they have laboriously composed. However, he finds that, embarrassingly, "all the bystanders might have explained the poems better than their authors could."[29] The poets, he concludes, don't use knowledge to write, but rather draw on an innate talent, or a well of inspiration from the muse. He compares the poets to the prophets, who similarly say things without necessarily understanding their significance. We have already discussed Nietzsche as a prophetic figure, but those who grapple with the aporia in his work read him more like an artist or poet than a philosopher. As Lefebvre writes, Nietzsche has been associated with "literary and poetic madness."[30]

In his 1967 essay "The Death of the Author," Barthes implicitly expands on this notion expressed by Socrates in the context of literary criticism. However, rather than point to the ignorance of the poet or writer in explaining their work, he criticises the methodological approach involved in turning to the author for the final word on a text's meaning. Barthes begins by quoting a phrase from one of Honoré de Balzac's stories, laced with misogynist undertones. He asks, "Who is speaking thus?"[31] The reader has several interpretive possibilities: the speaker might simply be the protagonist the line is attributed to, or perhaps the author himself, either channelling his own views or constructing certain "literary" ideas about women, or, alternatively, it may be a universal truth finding expression through this particular work. Barthes suggests that we cannot possibly arrive at a determinate answer, primarily because writing itself erodes the subject to whom we could address such a question. He argues that "writing is the destruction of every voice, of every point of origin."[32]

To understand this claim, we must look to the tendency Barthes writes *against*. He challenges a tradition that prioritises the biography of the writer, which characterises the dominant trend in Nietzsche scholarship. In this mode of interpretation, both representations and criticisms of works are inextricable from their makers. For example, "Baudelaire's work is the failure of Baudelaire the man, Van Gogh's his madness, Tchaikovsky's his vice."[33] Methodologically, then, the explanation of a particular text can be found by turning to the individual who produced it—by consulting the archive to decipher their beliefs and opinions. The period of focussing on the figure of the author is synonymous with a particularly fertile period for criticism. If an author can be "found" through an investigation into their personal history and context, then the text can be "explained," and the critic who has chosen the interpretive lens is the arbiter of its meaning.[34]

For Barthes, the author is ultimately a figure of modernity who emerges in tandem with capitalism and the rise of individualism. At other historical periods, we have related differently to reading as a society, and there are authors such as Proust and Mallarmé who have attempted to resist this biographical mode of reading through their writing practice. What Barthes terms the "scriptor" succeeds the author, and also produces a figure of the reader. This reader, as Barthes describes them, is altogether different from the critic. They have the capacity to maintain and navigate contradiction without capitulating to one fixed reading or another. To clarify this, Barthes points to Greek tragedy. He notes how tragedies often involved terms with double meanings in the course of the dialogue, resulting in misunderstandings or comedies of error that move the plot along. While only one sense of the word is available to the protagonist, the viewer holds space for both meanings. The viewer not only hears the dual implications of the word, but also perceives the "deafness" of the protagonist. The reader is the nexus where the multifarious interpretations that make up a text are "inscribed without any of them being lost."[35]

Barthes's division between the author and the scriptor-reader involves two different temporal experiences. In the paradigm which maintains the sovereignty of the author, the writer is situated "as the past of his own book."[36] We might think here again of Nietzsche's books as his progeny, as Barthes notes that in this reading, the figure of the author is "thought to *nourish* the book" in the way a father would his child.[37] The second paradigm removes the author as "predicate" to the text. Rather, each work is inscribed in the present anew with each reading. Barthes concludes, then, that when we approach a text, writing really takes place in the act of reading it, not at some determinate past point in which its author took up a pen.[38]

If we take Barthes's view, much of Nietzsche scholarship can be dismissed. "Once the Author is removed, the claim to decipher a text becomes quite futile. To give a text an author is to impose a limit on that text, to finish it with a final signified, to close the writing."[39] Barthes' analysis brings us back to the quasi-religious status of Nietzsche and his writings. If we accept this new understanding of a text, it is necessarily liberated from a determinate meaning. Barthes calls this the "message of the Author-God," or a "single 'theological' meaning."[40] Barthes would agree with the critic that a text is a tapestry of sources, contexts, quotations, and reverberations. However, he suggests that the concentration of this various parts is the reader, not the author.

In some ways, the trend in Nietzsche scholarship we have been addressing is one step ahead of "classical criticism," which Barthes reproves for only paying attention to the author and not the reader. Nietzsche scholars are obsessed with the derelict political subject Nietzsche's texts might produce if they fall into the wrong hands: if not a right-wing neo-fascist, then perhaps an anti-social person with destructive tendencies? Among the wave of Nietzsche criticism Fluss remarks on, many consider Nietzsche influential in the rise of far-right figures. Some of these thinkers openly name him as a direct influence: Richard Spencer, for example, admits to being "red-pilled by Nietzsche." Then there are historical oddities, like in 1924 when Nathan Leopold and Richard Loeb, two wealthy teenagers aged eighteen and nineteen years old, murdered a young boy at random without any motive beyond demonstrating their superior intellect. In his historical defence speech, Clarence Darrow says the following of Leopold:

> He became enamoured of the philosophy of Nietzsche. Your Honor, I have read almost everything that Nietzsche ever wrote. He was a man of a wonderful intellect; the most original philosopher of the last century . . . Nathan Leopold is not the only boy who has read Nietzsche. He may be the only one who was influenced in the way that he was influenced.

These individuals, who might easily be mistaken for readers of Nietzsche, are not true readers, at least in Barthes's sense of the word. In an altogether-less-academic context, they reproduce the same hermeneutic manoeuvre as the Nietzsche scholar by resolving Nietzsche's texts into one, prescriptible, and ultimately closed reading. With the death of the author—that is, the death of the historical Nietzsche—what is made possible in re-encountering his texts? With the birth of a different figure, the scriptor-Nietzsche, and his twin, the reader, a new hermeneutics emerges.

The Aesthetic Listener and Barthes's Reader in The (re-)Birth of Tragedy

There is an unmistakable resonance between the figure of the reader proposed in Barthes's account and what Nietzsche terms the "aesthetic listener" in *The Birth of Tragedy.* Without unproblematically taking Nietzsche at his word, we might be able to learn a hermeneutics from him that leads to better results than the approaches we have so far examined. Indeed, in the republication of the text in 1886 with the addition of the "Attempt at Self Criticism," Nietzsche stages an imagined dialogue with a reconstructed version of himself, whom he asks to listen with "a more attentive ear" to passages from *The Birth of Tragedy*. What is the "destiny" of the work according to Nietzsche's *own* practice of reading—not the Nietzsche of history, but the one that emerges from these texts themselves? Furthermore, if the approaches to Nietzsche scholarship we have discussed methodologically rely on a historical-biographical approach, they formally rely on a resolution of contradiction by omitting one of the terms of contradiction. In Nietzsche's own mixed reflections on his oeuvre and the relationship he proposes between the Apollonian and Dionysian, we find a different mode of negotiating contradiction than that practised by the cut-up artist.

There are many reasons why Nietzsche might not look back fondly on his first publication *The Birth of Tragedy.* Although he received positive feedback from the Wagners and the unacademic upper class in their milieu, and the text was *eventually* a bestseller, it had a very unfavourable initial reception. Of the eight hundred copies printed in 1872, only 625 were sold over the course of six years. Prideaux describes the work as "the suicide note of a philologist."[41] Of the critical silence from the educated world, Nietzsche comments that "it feels almost as though I had committed a crime."[42] The reviews that did come out were scathing. For instance, Nietzsche's professor, Friedrich Ritschl, described the text as "megalomaniac," and his colleague Jacob Burckhardt was "offended" by the work which was overwhelmingly "intemperate."[43] It irreparably damaged Nietzsche's reputation and institutional career. What's more, he eventually departed from his early celebratory characterisation of Wagner which is central to the text.

Surprisingly, Nietzsche comfortably maintains a positive, though nuanced, relationship to *The Birth of Tragedy*, both criticising and re-affirming it. We see this in both the "Attempt at Self-criticism" and *Ecce Homo*, which summarises Nietzsche's publication output in his own words. In the former, Nietzsche describes *The Birth of Tragedy* as "badly written, clumsy, embarrassing, furious, and frenzied."[44] But Nietzsche also suggests that his only regret is not having had the "sufficient courage and arrogance" to allow himself to express such personal and risky views in his own terms, instead of engaging with Arthur Schopenhauer and Immanuel Kant. So, while in some respects Nietzsche regrets the youthful awkwardness of this work, at least regarding style, he would double down on precisely what so many critics found objectionable about it—that is, its tendency to express Nietzsche's thoughts and opinions free from the conventions of academic referencing and engagement with other thinkers (especially philologists). In *Ecce Homo*, Nietzsche celebrates what was wrong with the book as having worked insofar as it had an effect. He says of the work, "This beginning is remarkable beyond all measure."[45] But he also points to its flaws, suggesting that it "made its *effect* and even exercised fascination through what was wrong with it," which, in this critique, is its focus on Wagner as a figure of cultural salvation.[46] This double manoeuvre of criticism and affirmation is true, in varying degrees, of many of his works and other aspects of his life reflected on in *Ecce Homo*. Contra the cut-up artist, then, Nietzsche cuts something out, only to paste it back where it originally was. Perhaps there is something like the art of kintsugi to the process—of mending with gold and highlighting the line of fracture.

In *The Birth of Tragedy*, the proposed relationship between the Apollonian and Dionysian points to a formal mode of understanding, a practice of resolving contradiction without cancelling out. Nietzsche equates the decline of modern music in opera with the decline of Greek tragedy. In the latter case, this is marked by Euripidean tragedy influenced by the Socratic tradition. Nietzsche identifies Wagner as a case of modern opera once again achieving something of the tragic that marked the height of Greek culture. For Nietzsche, the possibility of art itself hinges on the interplay between Apollonian and Dionysian forces, and *The Birth of Tragedy* is an inquiry into the nature of this union. The Apollonian is associated with form in art—for instance, in the practice of the sculptor—while the Dionysian relates to the formless and imageless medium of music. As psychological states, the Apollonian pertains to the dream and the Dionysian to intoxication. On the stage, where a tragedy is performed, the Apollonian is the "dream-world of the stage" and the Dionysian is the "lyric of the chorus."[47] Ultimately, Nietzsche argues that the Dionysian and Apollonian cannot be allowed to overtake one another or cancel each other out: the fusion of the Apollonian and Dionysian results in the transmissibility of the Dionysian *by virtue of* a certain submission to form through the Apollonian impulse.

Synonymous with the "rebirth of tragedy" is the emergence of the figure of the "aesthetic listener."[48] This listener stands in direct contrast to the figure of the "critic," which is not unlike Barthes's use of the term. For Nietzsche, the critic is characterised by "half moral and half scholarly pretensions," and is limited in what they are able to glean from aesthetic experience.[49] The aesthetic listener can extend themselves beyond the norms of their milieu and think outside the frameworks that they have been taught. Nietzsche measures the capacity of the aesthetic listener against their ability to engage emotionally with what takes place on stage. In doing so, they resolve the twofold experience of "seeing" and simultaneously "long[ing] for something beyond seeing."[50] Approaching Nietzsche like Barthes's "reader" or Nietzsche's "aesthetic listener" achieves a more productive relationship to his texts, avoiding the disorientation of reading Nietzsche selectively, as well as the inevitability of having to contend with ample evidence to the contrary of whatever interpretation with which we side. By refusing to resolve things for the reader, they are interpolated to confront for themselves the contradiction at hand. Precisely at the point where Nietzsche's output fails from the perspective of consistency, it most effectively works as an imperative to thought. Remember that the apocalyptic horror in William Yeats's poem *The Second Coming* begins with the falcon unable to hear the falconer. It is only when sound is lost over the "widening gyre" that "things fall apart; the centre cannot hold."

1 Susan Neuhaus, "Images of Service and Sacrifice: Tracing Narratives in Stained Glass," *Journal of Military and Veterans' Health* 26, no. 4 (2018): 27.
2 Kurt Tucholsky quoted in Domenico Losurdo, *Nietzsche, The Aristocratic Rebel: Intellectual Biography and Critical Balance-sheet*, trans. Gregor Benton (Brill, 2019), xiii.
3 Peter Sloterdijk, *Nietzsche Apostle*, trans. Stephen Corcoran (MIT Press, 2013), 71.
4 Sloterdijk, *Nietzsche*, 20.
5 Sloterdijk, 25.
6 Sue Prideaux, *I Am Dynamite!* (Faber & Faber, 2018), 372.
7 Prideaux, *Dynamite*, 142.
8 Joanne Faulkner, *Dead Letters to Nietzsche* (Ohio University Press, 2010), 4.
9 Prideaux, *Dynamite*, 369.
10 Prideaux, 368.
11 Prideaux, 327.
12 Prideaux, 327.
13 Geoff Waite, *Nietzsche's Corps/e* (Duke University Press, 1996), 15.
14 Prideaux, *Dynamite*, 120.
15 Stuart Elden. "Introduction: A Study of Productive Tensions," in Henri Lefebvre, *Metaphilosophy*, trans. David Fernbach, ed. Stuart Elden (Verso, 2016), x.
16 Losurdo, *Aristocratic Rebel*, 67.
17 Laurence Lampert, *What a Philosopher Is: Becoming Nietzsche* (The University of Chicago Press, 2017), 6.
18 Jennifer Ratner-Rosenhagen, *American Nietzsche: A History of an Icon and His Ideas* (The University of Chicago Press, 2012), 305.
19 Losurdo, *Aristocratic Rebel*, 1008.
20 Losurdo, 1008.
21 Losurdo, 1008.
22 Sloterdijk, *Nietzsche Apostle*, 6–7.
23 Michel Foucault, "Prison Talk," interview by Jean-Jacques Brochier, in *Power and Knowledge*, ed. Colin Gordon (Harvester Press, 1980), 534.
24 Prideaux, *Dynamite*, 374–5.
25 Prideaux, 375.
26 Prideaux, 39.
27 Prideaux, 40.
28 Prideaux, 72–3.
29 Plato, "Apology," in *Plato: Complete Works*, ed. John M. Cooper, trans. George M. A. Grube (Hackett Publishing Company, 1997), 22.
30 Henri Lefebvre, *Hegel, Marx, Nietzsche* trans. David Fernbach (Verso, 2020), np.
31 Roland Barthes, "The Death of the Author," in *Image, Music, Text*, trans. Stephen Heath (Fontana, 1977), 142.
32 Barthes, "The Death of the Author," 142.
33 Barthes, 143.
34 Barthes, 147.
35 Barthes, 148.
36 Barthes, 146.

37 Barthes, 146.
38 Barthes, 147.
39 Barthes, 147.
40 Barthes, 146.
41 Prideaux, *Dynamite,* 111.
42 Prideaux, 99.
43 Prideaux, 106.
44 Friedrich Nietzsche, *The Birth of Tragedy,* trans. Douglas Smith (Oxford University Press, 2000), 5.
45 Friedrich Nietzsche, *Ecce Homo,* trans. Reginald J. Hollingdale (Penguin, 2004), 49.
46 Nietzsche, *Ecce Homo,* 48.
47 Nietzsche, *Birth*, 52.
48 Nietzsche, 120.
49 Nietzsche, 120.
50 Nietzsche, 127.

The Forced Choice of Post-Modernism: Alenka Zupančič's Nietzsche

Rex Butler

The Forced Choice of Post-Modernism

Undoubtedly, the popular image of philosophy is as the referee and gatekeeper of all the disciplines. It is what sets the test for their truth claims, while not putting forward any itself. It is not a science or a history or even an art, but what judges the validity, usefulness, and truthfulness of these. It is modest and self-questioning, and seeks to make modest those others, which are always tempted to overstep their mark and make assertions they should not in a language that is not properly theirs. The defining word here is Karl Popper's "falsifiability": his notion that this philosophical testing means that the truthfulness of any statement is possible only insofar as it is potentially falsifiable, and for this reason all such statements can only be provisionally true while awaiting their future falsification.[1] The history of thought is a series of incremental advances that never attain the final truth, and, in a way, one even knows in advance, at least if they have read Popper, that they will never get to this final truth, insofar as their falsification will inevitably come before that. But what if philosophy were not like this? What if philosophy—and this would be what defines it—is characterised by statements that cannot be refuted, cannot be judged against some pre-existing reality, but on the contrary make their own reality? What if what characterises a proper philosophical statement is that it is irrefutable, insofar as there is nothing outside it to which it can be compared, but also undemonstrable, insofar as there is no evidence we can bring to it that is not already an effect of it? What if, paradoxically, philosophy *doubled* the world, at once repeating it in a perfect description and bringing it about in an unprecedented prescription? What if the world philosophy spoke of did not exist before it, but after what it says it has always existed, and philosophy is merely recounting what is already there?

We can say that all philosophy is like this, but if we had to name the one philosopher who most explicitly makes this clear, it would be Friedrich Nietzsche. It is Nietzsche who speaks of philosophy as "breaking the world in two," and who conducts his argument not as any kind of rational discourse employing evidence or even persuasion,[2] but through his famous "aphoristic" style or method, in which a series of short or abrupt assertions are either immediately accepted or not.

Or perhaps more accurately—if one follows him at all—statements that cannot but be believed, that once said make themselves true.[3] And, of course, at this point there is raised the complex question of what it is to "follow" Nietzsche. For our purposes, we suggest that, if one does not "follow" him, one does not even recognise his statements, and they are not even statements until they are followed. There is thus an absolute "materiality" to Nietzsche's discourse, not in the sense that it can be formally analysed for its tone, style, or influence—these are secondary and come only afterwards—but in the sense that it *is* what it speaks of. The literal words or marks on the page are a kind of event that changes everything. They open up a break between the before and the after, precisely with the result that there is no "before" to Nietzsche's statements: the world they speak of does not exist before them, or this world that exists before them is also only an effect of them. In this sense, even to be indifferent to or unaware of Nietzsche can only be explained because of him, is only deliberately to ignore him. Nietzsche speaks of his philosophy and philosophy in general as coming out of the "stillest hour,"[4] and by this he might be said to mean that nothing predicts or explains the "event" it represents. There is no cause in the world, no influence in history, no particular intellectual history or background that accounts for it more than any other. A proper philosophical statement comes out of nothing and brings about its world. And everything that would explain it, that world to which it is faithful, is merely its consequence.

In this essay, we want to look at Nietzsche and his "influence" on philosophy. In particular, we want to look, if only briefly and suggestive of further work, at the "influence" of Nietzsche on a generation of French thinkers who were influential in Australia in the 1980s and made up the intellectual movement known as "post-modernism," or more colloquially "French theory." We speak of Jacques Derrida, Gilles Deleuze, Jean Baudrillard, and Jean-François Lyotard, although there are any number of others we could include. However, ultimately we would want to say that, to the extent that we properly understand Nietzsche and take his arguments seriously, the *entire* history of philosophy after Nietzsche is Nietzschean, as is now perhaps the *entire* history of philosophy before him.

Nietzsche introduces a logic or method—both these terms need to be understood in inverted commas—that henceforth defines significant philosophy. But, again, it is not a question of influence or of some identifiable method that is consciously shared. If one is to be a proper "Nietzschean" philosopher, one has to begin from nothing like him, not describing or accounting for some pre-existing world, but bringing one about. If there is a lineage of Nietzschean philosophy, it is a history of singularities, and if the philosophers we speak of invoke Nietzsche as an "influence," they each create a different Nietzsche. Indeed, they each break with Nietzsche, offer a different "doubling" explanation of him. But it is also therefore Nietzsche who is each time the "same," insofar as, to be a proper Nietzschean philosopher, one has to enact the same "doubling" as him. Each time, in a history of Nietzschean philosophy, we begin again from the beginning. There is no history, therefore, of Nietzschean philosophy, but rather what we might call an Eternal Return: a repetition of what has come before, but with what comes before existing only after it has been repeated.

How to characterise in more detail this defining Nietzschean gesture? As we say, we could begin anywhere, insofar as after him all significant thought is a version of it, but we might start here with Slovenian philosopher and literary theorist Alenka Zupančič's *The Shortest Shadow: Nietzsche's Philosophy of the Two* (2003). In particular, we might open with a certain moment, one after which her book is named and that she sees as "central" to Nietzsche's method. She tracks it at greatest length in the section "Noon" of her book, which occurs almost at its midway point, but she earlier raises it in relation to a passage from Nietzsche's *The Twilight of the Idols* (1889). In the passage in question, Nietzsche postulates a certain *Schatten* or shadow that can be seen at midday, exactly when the sun is at its highest and there should be no shadow. In Nietzsche's own abbreviated German: "*Mittag, Augenblick des kürzesten Schattens; Ende des längsten Irrthums;*

Höhepunkt der Menschheit." Or in R. J. Hollingdale's well-known English translation, which Zupančič uses: "Mid-day; moment of the shortest shadow; end of the longest error; zenith of mankind."[5] What is the point Nietzsche is making here? It is sometimes thought that he is positing an actual shadow at midday, as though the light does not illuminate all and something remains obscure. It would be as though this shadow were an alternative to light, and that within this shadow we would find something hidden if only we looked more closely. But this is not it at all. In fact, Nietzsche emphasises that, at midday, the light illuminates *everything* and there is no shadow. And he is speaking of that "shadow" that ensures everything is illuminated and there is no shadow.

But what does Nietzsche mean by this? In what sense can he be referring to shadow if there is no actual shadow? What kind of shadow can remain when the sun is at its highest and everything is illuminated? It is here that we get to the heart of Nietzsche's method, at least according to Zupančič. We might begin by thinking what he means by speaking of his philosophy "breaking the world in two," which would produce not just a before and an after, but a split or division occurring in the present. It would be not just a getting lighter in the morning and a getting darker in the evening, but a separation of every moment from itself. When Nietzsche speaks of midday being the time of the "shortest shadow," he is not referring to any actual shadow, some shadow that is able to be seen. In a way, that would still only be light. It would be a shadow that is visible, and thus not truly in shadow. Rather, he is speaking of a "shadow" that *allows* the light, indeed, the very opposition between light and shadow, which allows everything to be seen. He is speaking of a "shadow" that means there is no shadow. In this sense, it is a shadow that is split from itself, that on the one hand is an actual shadow in the world that can be seen and on the other the "shadow" that precedes or is outside the world that makes all things visible. To use a recognisable philosophical language, we might say that this "shadow" is the transcendental condition of light, of seeing the world; but unlike Kant's transcendental condition it is not simply outside the world, existing in itself, but also part of it, only able to be named and thought as an object and in a language that is familiar to us. In this sense, this "shadow" is unable to be seen, exists only as a thought, or, perhaps more accurately, as a result of Nietzsche's statement—which, beautifully, is only a series of black marks on a white page—but, after it, the statement cannot be denied, for its very absence is its proof. And yet again—and this goes towards the idea that this statement also brings about the very world it speaks of—it is nothing other than the world. The world as such is its own shadow, stands in for its shadow, which is also nothing else outside of it, being merely another shadow in the world.

Zupančič makes a brilliant comparison at one point between what Nietzsche is saying and the Russian Constructivist Kazimir Malevich's *Black Square* (1915), which is often said to be the first truly abstract painting. In *Black Square*, we have a simple black square placed evenly and symmetrically on a plain white surface, and Zupančič speaks of it as the "first 'content' or object created by painting *from within its own practice*."[6] Zupančič then a few pages later goes on to make a comparison with Malevich's later *Suprematist Composition: White on White* (1918), in which there is not a black square on a white background but a white square on a white background, distinguishable only by its slightly more gestural brushstrokes to mark it out. And what she says of *White on White* is that it figures that "moment when 'One turns to Two,' namely, the very moment of a break or split."[7] Her point, of course, is that what we have in *White on White* is something like that "shortest shadow" elaborated in *The Twilight of the Idols*, in which there is a kind of invisible split in the white, or the brightness of the day is only possible, or only visible, because of a certain invisible shadow for which both the light and the shadow stand in. In this sense, *White on White* can be understood as the ultimate consequence of that break in *Black Square*, in which the "shadow" produced by the division between black and white means that everything is illuminated, including shadow, which becomes another form of light. And yet, in another way, *Black Square* does remain the foundational painting,

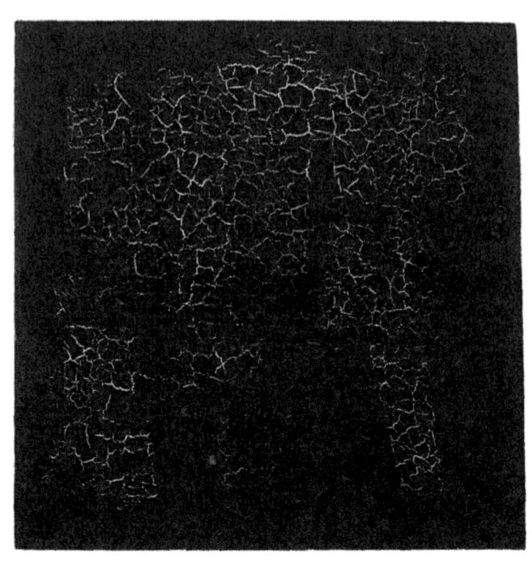

Kazimir Malevich, *Black Suprematist Square*, 1915,
oil on canvas, 79.5 × 79.5 cm.

Kazimir Malevich, *Suprematist Composition: White on White*, 1918, oil on canvas, 79.4 × 79.4 cm.

insofar as it is the split between black and black, the actual shadow and that invisible shadow for which it stands in and that allows it to be seen, that allows light or the split between light and shadow. It is the split within the black square in *Black Square*, we might say, that produces the effect of that black square on a white background and everything else that comes after it in the history of art.

Forced Choice

In fact, much of *The Shortest Shadow* is concerned with the great Nietzschean question of "nihilism," which has been addressed by any number of his interpreters, most notably Martin Heidegger and Elisabeth Kuhn. In the first section of the book, "Nietzsche the Metapsychologist," we have Nietzsche on the "psychology"—really, the psychoanalysis—of nihilism. Then, in the second section, "Noon," we have him on the notion of "Nothing," at first as "double affirmation" and then as "minimal difference," as though it were the "solution" to the problem of nihilism after the "still point" of noon at the centre. But how is this so? How does this actually play out in Zupančič's book (although, again, it is never quite the "argument" of Nietzsche, if we mean by that the logical elaboration of a proposition that is meant rationally to persuade us)? And it is here that we come to the other half of the title of our essay, "forced choice," with the argument that philosophy does not simply oppose the "forced choice" that characterises contemporary society by offering another choice, but seeks to go beyond it by replaying it, by thinking that "forced choice" that precedes and makes possible this forced choice, as it were. Again—and this is how he goes against the conventional understanding of philosophy—Nietzsche does not seek to offer an alternative to what is that we can decide to choose, which will only turn back into it, but seeks to think its conditions of possibility, which we cannot but choose. Now, admittedly, any stated condition of possibility is also only able to be thought in terms of what it allows, and thus turns back into it, but philosophy is able to think *this* and therefore think that "shadow" that precedes the very distinction between light and shadow, things and what allows them to be seen.

Of course, Nietzsche is perhaps best known for his apparent critique of and opposition to religion, particularly the Christian religion. "Antichrist," "Dionysius against the Crucified," and "God is dead, and we have killed him" are some characterisations and self-characterisations that have entered our culture and shaped our image of Nietzsche. But this notion of Nietzsche "opposing" religion is too simple, and Nietzsche rather confronts the fact that there is no alternative to religion—or religion, especially after the European Enlightenment, is already its own alternative. (Indeed, as Zupančič says, it is the Christian religion itself, or one of its alternatives, that already says "God is dead" before Nietzsche.[8]) In fact, Nietzsche's critique of Christianity is an unexpected one: it is that, against the idea that religion offers us hope and redemption in a world full of sin and suffering, it is actually nihilistic. But this nihilism must be understood as not the absence of meaning, but its abundance and even superfluidity. Nihilism for Nietzsche—and we will come to see how religion is implicated in this—is not so much the loss or absence of meaning as the very search for and even finding of meaning.[9]

Let us begin with Catholicism, the "original" Christian religion. Catholicism is, of course, the great religion of ritual and ceremony. The priests in their robes that separate them from us mediate between us and God. Indeed, the priest and his ceremony *is* God. God is His symbolic ritual, and this can even be understood in the Lacanian sense of the symbolic bringing about God. As a result, it is a matter of us believing not directly in God but rather in the designated officials of the Church, who believe for us. And at this point, according to Nietzsche, there occurs a parodying and emptying out of all authentic "religious" values. For as long as we appear to follow the outward rituals of the Church, it doesn't matter what we inwardly believe. Indeed, the Church ultimately doesn't want us to believe—that would only complicate things—but merely to follow the official protocols and leave it to others to believe on our behalf. We do not will something, but rather no longer will. This is Zupančič on what she calls the "passive nihilism" of Catholicism:

> Within classical Catholicism, the clear distinction between here and beyond, this world and the other world, depends largely upon the power of the Symbolic to be the mediator or common ground of the two. Symbolic rituals accompanying certain actions and commitments in this world have the power to transform these actions and commitments into something that simultaneously takes place in the other world.[10]

In response to this passive "not willing" of Catholicism, the Church "reforms" itself in that form of Christianity known as Protestantism. Protestantism, in a kind of transcendental critique of Catholicism, seeks to strip away all the earthly ceremonies and authorised mediators that come between us and God and get directly to God Himself. Or, to put it another way, against that reduction of God to the symbolic, Protestantism wishes to place God beyond us and our worldly projections. In a way, the paradox of Protestantism is that it wants to have a direct or unmediated relationship with God in which it is a matter of our personal belief, as though He would not exist outside of it, and yet God must also always remain unknown, with none of our earthly actions having any bearing on our eventual heavenly fate.

This is the famous contradiction pointed out by German sociologist Max Weber in his *The Protestant Ethic and the Spirit of Capitalism*: that our destiny has already been decided, and we can do nothing about it, though this does not lead to any passivity, but to the endless undertaking of good works and accumulation of wealth.[11] However, these are not the attempts to change our destiny, but the expression of this destiny, so many efforts to live up to it. Instead of the "not willing" of Catholicism, we now have—in another form of that "nihilism" Nietzsche says characterises Christianity—a "willing of Nothing" that directly tries to capture God in His failure to be represented. This is Zupančič on this second moment of Christianity:

> One could define the central project of the Reformation precisely as an attempt to "(re)activate God"—this time not as the power of the Symbolic, but as an immediate power of the Real. God (as real) and our proximity to Him are now explicitly situated beyond the Symbolic, namely, beyond the logic of mediation, representation, and hierarchy.[12]

What, ultimately, is that "nihilism" that Nietzsche diagnoses in Christianity? In Catholicism, we have a certain "not willing," a deliberate giving up of one's own will or desire and a delegating of it to others. It is what Nietzsche calls "passive nihilism." In Protestantism, we have an attempt to overcome this passivity and take things into our own hands by directly relating to God Himself outside His earthly ceremonies and designated mediators. He would be what lies outside the symbolic order, whether this is understood as the Church or the very order of meaning and language. And in this willing of a certain "Nothing," Protestantism understands itself as a solution to the "not willing" of Catholicism. But in Protestantism we would always fall short of and miss that God we aim at, impose on Him something familiar and recognisable to ourselves, and have to start again. We see this in both those incessantly renewed tasks in Weber's "work ethic" and in something like anorexia, where whatever we eat only stands in for the true pleasure of eating, and we have to be even more strict in our diet.[13] And this would be that "active nihilism" that Nietzsche diagnoses in Protestantism in its attempt to propose a corrective to Catholicism. But, in fact, the true nihilism that Nietzsche diagnoses is not so much either one of these alternatives, as the fact that Christianity proposes its own alternative and there is therefore no true alternative to Christianity. Protestantism presents itself as the alternative to Catholicism in speaking of the true and unattainable God that lies behind it and makes it possible, but its incessant failed attempts actually to think and name that Nothing lead to us giving up and once again leaving our belief in the hands of others. So that, if Christianity appears to offer us a choice—and Protestantism in its "reform" of Christianity does not simply want to do away with Catholicism, but rather leave the choice in our hands as a test of our faith—it is not a true choice, but a false or "forced choice," with each alternative ultimately inseparable from the other. The "not willing" of Catholicism is not possible outside the "Nothing" of Protestantism, and the attempt to think the "Nothing" of Protestantism ultimately turns into the "not willing" of Catholicism.

Zupančič uses the phrase "forced choice" towards the end of her book precisely with regard to this apparent choice between passive nihilism and active nihilism, "not willing" and "willing Nothing." As she writes: "Clearly, for Nietzsche, both alternatives are, so to speak, 'worse' . . . As I have already pointed out, nihilism is what sets before us this forced choice: 'to will nothingness or not to will.'"[14] But, in fact, the concept of "forced choice" was first theorised by Lacan in his seminar *The Four Fundamentals of Psychoanalysis* and later in *Ou pire*... For Lacan, the "forced choice" is a consequence of us entering the symbolic order, in which things have meaning only in their differential relationship to each other and the Real is excluded. As Lacan writes in *The Four Fundamentals*: "The *vel* [either/or] of alienation is defined by a choice whose properties depend on this, that there is, in the joining [with the symbolic order], some element that, whatever the choice operating may be, has as its consequence a *neither one nor the other*."[15] But it is perhaps Slavoj Žižek who does the most to popularise the concept and demonstrate its relevance to contemporary society. He will speak, for example, of the proliferation of apparent consumer "choices"—for example, that between Coke and Pepsi—which, if appearing to offer us a form of consumerist self-expression, also remind us that any real satisfaction of need is excluded by our entering into the symbolic, and all we now have is a sign of need and a sign of satisfaction: "The ever-present alternative to Nutra-Sweet Equal and High & Low, where almost everyone has his or her preference, and this ridiculous sticking to one's choice, only accentuates the meaninglessness of the alternative."[16]

But if these examples are undoubtedly comic, Žižek once got into serious trouble, and went close to being that mythical word "cancelled," for his proposal that in the 2016 United States presidential election voters—and by this Žižek meant his usual Left constituency—consider Donald Trump over Hillary Clinton. His undoubtedly provocative point was that this is not merely some protest against a false Leftist in Clinton, but rather that in our modern Western democratic systems there is no real choice between the inevitable two political parties representing Left and Right, which at the same time as appearing to cover all alternatives define themselves in relation to each other. Precisely what gets left out is any alternative, so that effectively a vote for Clinton *is* a vote for Trump, and it is just this false choice that Žižek wants to make us think by a refusal that can nevertheless only take the form of one of these alternatives. This is Žižek in "Clinton, Trump and the Left's Dilemma": "They are both worse! Trump is obviously 'worse.' He enacts a decay of public morality. He promises a Rightist turn. But at least he promises change. Hilary is 'worse,' since she makes changing nothing look desirable."[17] And, of course, the fact that in 2024 there will be a second runoff between Joe Biden and Trump demonstrates that a vote for Clinton would not have got rid of Trump and that no matter what choice we make the same alternative will keep coming back.

What, then, is Nietzsche's "solution" to the problem of the forced choice? How can he be "critical" of Christianity if Christianity is already critical of itself? How can he offer an "alternative" to Catholicism and Protestantism when each is the only alternative to the other? The first point to make is that Nietzsche is not simply critical of Christianity, and does not seek to offer an alternative to its forced choice. Indeed, we might even say the opposite: Nietzsche wants to think about what makes Christianity necessary, and that there is only this forced choice. How so? At one point in *The Shortest Shadow*, Zupančič speaks of a famous philosophical problem called the liar paradox. It was first proposed by the Ancient Greek philosopher Epimenides, and it concerns the status of the statement "I am lying." There seem to be two possible responses to this: either to suggest that this statement is itself a lie, so that there is no possible truth, or that to the very extent that this is the case there must be an exception, some higher place from where we can truthfully say that this is a lie.

But of course—and this is the great challenge that Epimenides set philosophy—for all the apparent opposition between the two positions, they are inseparable from each other: we cannot say that there is no truth except from a position of truth, but also this apparent exception cannot be thought or acted upon without turning back into a lie. But Zupančič then remarks that, if this choice has structured philosophical discourse for millennia, Lacan for his part suggests that we negotiate the apparently stark alternative between truth and lies, speech and meta-speech, all the time in our everyday lives:

> We have to pay attention to the fact that the statement that is thus excluded in logic ("the third possibility") is not something between truth and falsehood; it is not a half-truth, but, precisely, the point where we are uttering a truth in a way that we are *simultaneously* saying something about this utterance. It is by excluding this possibility (that, in stating something, we are also stating the value of this statement) that the strict dichotomy between a truth and a lie is established.[18]

How might this be thought in terms of Nietzsche's "overcoming" of the nihilism of Christianity? Along the lines of those two responses to the liar paradox, we have a God that is only the symbolic in Catholicism and a God that is beyond the symbolic in Protestantism. In the first, God is dead and something of a lie, and in the second, He is an unattainable higher truth that judges all else to be a lie. But "before" this, what makes not so much each alternative possible—because each in fact makes the other possible—but the very choice between them possible is a God that is *at once* immanent and transcendental, a lie and a higher truth, a God that is simultaneously Himself and about Himself. And to think this God is to think the forced choice between Catholicism and Protestantism, as though the choice had not yet been made. Or it would be to think its necessity, which means that there is only this alternative, but in thinking it, opens it up to a kind of contingency—even though the very split of God, the fact that He is simultaneously immanent and transcendent, a lie and the truth, can only take the form of one of His alternatives.

What Nietzsche is thinking, in other words, is that this forced choice would not take place without us, without the split that is our thinking of it. This is why Nietzsche's philosophy is not critical or negative, but positive and affirmative, does not oppose a "No" to a "Yes," but adds a "Yes" to a "Yes," while at the same time thinking that this first "Yes," that of the forced choice, would not exist without that second "Yes," which is our completely free thinking of it.[19] And this is also why, when Nietzsche speaks of himself as "Dionysius," as opposed to the "Crucified," this "Dionysius" does not simply exist outside the "Crucified," but is only the split within it, as he is thereby the split in himself.[20] And this is the Real that God is: not a Real that exists outside the symbolic as some "Nothing" that everything falls short of, but a Real that is only the split within things, including within itself.

Post-Modernism

Philosophy, proper philosophy, like Nietzsche's Antichrist, introduces a gap between things and themselves. It proposes a transcendental condition for things, which explains why they are as they are, and it is only those things themselves. Zupančič speaks here—and, of course, this whole question of positing the transcendental conditions of things is Kantian—of the way that Kant would call this a "transcendental illusion," the mistaken naming of the transcendental in terms of what it allows, but precisely for Zupančič this is all that is possible: "This indicates, perhaps, the unique possibility of perceiving something that is not an object of experience, but is also *not* the noumenon, the 'Thing in itself.'"[21] (And there is a whole thread of discussion in Zupančič about the inseparability of the "sublimated" and the "desublimated": the way that the most sublime and immaterial can only be grasped through the lowest and material, and the lowest and material, when thought about properly, reveal the sublime and immaterial.[22]) And perhaps in terms of this "transcendental" for which things stand in, it is the occasion to think the place of Nietzsche in all we are saying here. For, in one way, it is *Nietzsche* who initiates all of this, who is that thinker for whom all others stand in, and who lies at the origin of that history we are about to sketch. It would be that model of the unwavering transmission of thought that we see in the Lacanian procedure of *la passe*, in which training analysts do not pass on their findings directly but to two interlocutors, who then pass them on to the examining committee, as though to pare them down to what cannot be lost or misunderstood. But at the same time—and this is also the lesson of *la passe*—each thinker we speak of, and thought in general, must begin from "nothing," and the only thing that is passed on is the difference from one to the other. There is nothing before them, or what is "before" them is only the effect of that doubling transcendental statement they introduce into things. Which is also to say—and Zupančič paradoxically makes this clear—that there can be no overview of all this, no external perspective from which to survey this history and speak of it.[23] If what we are writing here is to mean anything, it must itself—as Zupančič does with her Nietzsche— "double" what comes before it, so that everything we speak of is only an effect of our own transcendental explanation.

To begin our "history," we start with Derrida. For is not Derrida's notion of "différance" precisely like that "shadow" at midday spoken of by Nietzsche? That is, against certain readings of his work, Derrida is not simply opposed to presence. His différance is not an absence that stands against presence. Rather—in a logic that should be familiar to us by now—différance is what allows presence, and is even what ensures there is *only* presence, so that différance itself can only ever be seen through presence. As Derrida repeatedly makes clear, aware as he is of the failure of others to do this, any attempt to name an alternative to the metaphysical systems of presence is only to miss it, to choose their aporetic other in a false forced choice. But Derrida also wants to make us think about this forced choice between absence and presence, in which each is only possible because of the other, and the real difference is what lies between them—

différance being only nameable in terms of a metaphysical system, and what makes this system possible is first of all its own difference from itself. Accordingly, then, Derrida's readings of specific metaphysical systems—and his work each time engages with a particular philosophical text, speaking in its own language—are at once all the same and all different. They are ungeneralisable, do not form any consistent method, and yet, as an essay like "Of an Apocalyptic Tone Recently Adopted in Philosophy" demonstrates, différance is more "transcendental" than even Kant's transcendentals in making transcendentality itself possible.[24] Altogether we would say that we have in Derrida a philosophical *drive* that is the continuous and unself-conscious attempt to state the transcendental conditions of thinking, without knowing in advance that it will fail and a certain différance will arise out of this failure. And this drive, this self-splitting, is why Derrida continues to use the word "différance" throughout his career, without seeking to go higher and speaking about its failure from somewhere else. Here is Derrida on his choice of the word "sign," for example:

> There is no sense in doing without the concepts of metaphysics in order to shake metaphysics. We have no language—no syntax and no lexicon—which is foreign to this history; we can pronounce not a single destructive proposition which has not already had to slip into the form, the logic, and the implicit postulations of precisely what it seeks to contest . . . But, as I suggested a moment ago, as soon as one seeks to demonstrate in this way that there is no transcendental or privileged signified and that the domain or play of signification henceforth has no limit, one must reject even the concept and word "sign" itself—which is precisely what cannot be done.[25]

We see much the same thing—indeed, exactly the same thing—in Deleuze. Of course, we could read his *Nietzsche and Philosophy* to demonstrate that he is making the same argument as Zupančič, or Zupančič is making the same argument as him (which on occasions she comes close to admitting[26]).

This is not merely because both are writing on the same Nietzsche, but because both are the same Nietzscheans. And, like Derrida, Deleuze repeats this same "Nietzschean" logic no matter what he writes about, even if it is not Nietzsche. Let us just take the argument from his and Félix Guattari's *Anti-Oedipus* and its sequel *A Thousand Plateaus*. As with Derrida, it is sometimes suggested—it can even appear this way from certain remarks by Deleuze and Guattari themselves—that "deterritorialisation" is simply opposed to capitalism and its reterritorialisation (and, certainly, within the forced choice of capitalism, it is). But, at the same time, deterritorialisation is the condition of possibility of reterritorialisation, what means there is *only* reterritorialisation. In this case, for all of the apparently liberatory "desire" they argue for, there is something of the same "pessimism" as Nietzsche, insofar as they propose neither a new centre nor a doing away with of existing centres. And neither is it a matter of successive deterritorialisations, each building on the one before, which as we have seen would soon run out of energy. Rather, deterritorialisation *doubles* reterritorialisation, is the shadow to its light, turning one into two. The real force behind Deleuze and Guattari's work, therefore, would be *drive*, not desire, the thinking of the forced choice between deterritorialisation and reterritorialisation, and the way neither would be possible without the other. Here is a passage from *A Thousand Plateaus* in which Deleuze and Guattari speak of the way that deterritorialisation is not an other to reterritorialisation, but opens up a split within it by first of all being a split from itself (deterritorialisation "deterritorialises" itself):

> Each of these becomings [the wasp and the orchid] brings about the deterritorialisation of one term and the reterritorialisation of the other; the two becomings interlink and form relays in a circulation of intensities pushing the deterritorialisation ever further. There is neither imitation nor resemblance, only an exploding of two heterogeneous series on the line of flight composed by a common rhizome that can no longer be attributed to or subjugated by anything signifying.[27]

Next, we might look at a thinker who is not often compared to Derrida and Deleuze, who is seen as not only not a "philosopher" like them but also as intellectually opposed to them (nihilistic as opposed to utopian, pessimistic as opposed to optimistic, conservative as opposed to radical): Baudrillard. But we want to insist that they are not merely comparable, but entirely the same (and Baudrillard, for his part, like Derrida and Deleuze, absolutely admits the foundational "influence" of Nietzsche[28]). And Baudrillard too—as though to prove their identity—is subject to the same kinds of misreadings as Derrida and Deleuze. We see this, for example, in the film *The Matrix*, said to be inspired by his work, in which "simulation" is understood to be some simple alternative to reality (the blue pill as opposed to the red pill). But simulation does not contest reality in suggesting that it is false or fictional. On the contrary, to put this in its strongest possible terms, simulation just *is* reality, and even what makes reality possible. Indeed, it is what ensures that there is *only* reality, and that all alternatives turn back into reality. But simulation is also that shadow at the brightest height of reality, and Baudrillard makes this Nietzschean point apparent in his *In the Shadow of the Silent Majorities*, in which, at the same time as the "masses" are endlessly polled and surveyed so that we know everything about them, they are also entirely unknown and unpredictable. (Shades of those "masses" behind Trump.) And it is these "masses" that constitute a kind of internal limit to both the social and society, at once allowing them to expand endlessly and ensuring that they are never total and have no real idea about those people they speak of and incorporate. Against orthodox readings, Baudrillard's work is not an attack upon but a defence of the real, but this "real" might be understood in the Lacanian sense: not as something directly obtained (in this case, it would be merely another simulation), but as something always split from itself, between it and its simulation, we might say. In other words, what is "real" in Baudrillard is not any alternative to simulation, but the fact that, thanks to simulation, there is only reality. A certain gap is opened up between reality and itself that is the "real" of simulation. As Baudrillard writes in *In the Shadow*:

> The mass is without attribute, predicate, quality, reference. This is its definition, or its radical lack of definition . . . Any attempt to qualify [the mass] only seeks to transfer it back to sociology and rescue it from this indistinctness, which is not even that of equivalence (the unlimited sum of equivalent individuals: 1 + 1 + 1—such is the sociological definition), but that of the *neutral*, which is to say *neither one nor the other* (ne-uter).[29]

Perhaps as a last example—although our point would be that all proper systems of thought are like this—we might speak of Lyotard and his notion of "post-modernism," developed in a series of books and essays from the late seventies and early eighties. Of course, in one way, post-modernism can be seen as an actual historical and cultural moment in a linear continuum. Viewed in this light, Lyotard can be seen to be amongst the first to theorise the concept, although for others it would be Fredric Jameson, and for us Australians, even Bernard Smith. The caveat is then added that this post-modernism is also the end of this linear thinking, or the so-called grand narratives. But for Lyotard, the post-modern does not so much come after the modern and mark its end, as *before* it and make it possible. For Lyotard, the incessant "presentation" of the modern arrives to take the place of the "unpresentable" of the post-modern. If post-modernism is an alternative to the modern, it also opens up the very alternative between the modern and the post-modern. There is only modernism—to the extent that post-modernism marks the end of the modern, it would only be the next modernist moment—but this only because of the post-modern. And Lyotard speaks of this in terms of Kant's sublime, but, as opposed to Kant's sublime, in which another higher transcendental is brought about in the ability to think the failure of the previous transcendental in that kind of Enlightenment recursion we previously looked at with regard to Protestantism. Lyotard speaks of an "immanence," in which the sublime just *is* this split between the presented and the unpresentable, its failure to be thought without another "outside" position being implied by this.[30] This is Lyotard in "Answering the Question: What is Post-Modernism?" on this split between the world and itself, its thinking and its inability to be thought, that is the post-modern sublime:

> The postmodern would be that which, in the modern, puts forward the unpresentable in presentation itself . . . The artist and the writer, then, are working without rules in order to formulate the rules of what *will have been done*. Hence the fact that work and text have the characters of an *event*; hence, also, they always come too late for their author, or, what amounts to the same thing, their being put into work, their realisation, always begins too soon. *Post modern* would have to be understood according to the paradox of future (*post*) anterior (*modo*).[31]

Every thinker after Nietzsche—and, of course, now before Nietzsche—has to bring about the "same" doubling of the world: introduce a transcendental condition that at once explains everything and is no different from what it explains (différance, deterritorialisation, simulation, the post-modern sublime). Each has to follow Nietzsche, and can be seen to be repeating him, and yet also has to start from nothing, that "stillest hour," so that nothing comes before them, and they create their world. Each accounts for all the others (and Nietzsche), and each is also exactly like those others (and Nietzsche). In a way, we come back each time to the beginning, in a kind of Eternal Return that, as Zupančič makes clear—and as we see in a figure like Sarah Connor at the end of *The Terminator*—at once enacts a perfect fated circle and is only possible because of something outside that circle. Each great philosopher disappears into what they have created, is merely an effect of the sources, influences, and other great philosophers that have come before them, and yet all of this is only because of them, who also stands outside of this, absolutely unique and inexplicable. It is again what Zupančič means by Nietzsche's philosophy being not negative but doubly affirmative, adding a "Yes" to a "Yes." Each only repeats the forced choice of their world, but this forced choice would not exist without them. But in a way what cannot be seen by each philosopher, like Freud not recognising himself in the mirror in the experience of the "uncanny," is themself in their world. They can propose their doubling hypothesis from somewhere outside, and they can see the world their hypothesis has made, but they cannot see or speak of their hypothesis actually making the world, which is also the very "gap" between their hypothesis and the world. This is why Zupančič can speak of the proper tense of philosophy being the "future anterior," and why there cannot be any "objective" overview or assessment of what we are speaking of here, as philosophy proposed at the beginning of our paper.[32] But "Nietzsche" is the name for this gap, this shadow, this midday, at once connecting and separating the before and the after. It is Nietzsche who allows us to think (and to think that we cannot think) this moment of doubling. The "event" Nietzsche is the very difference between Nietzsche and Zupančič, Zupančič and herself, and Zupančič and me, if what I have to say here is to count at all.

1 See on this the chapter "Falsifiability," in Karl Popper, *The Logic of Scientific Discovery* (Routledge, 2002), 57–73.
2 Alenka Zupančič, *The Shortest Shadow: Nietzsche's Philosophy of the Two* (MIT Press, 2003), 9.
3 Zupančič speaks, following Alain Badiou, of the connection—indeed, the equivalence—between the Nietzschean "declaration" and the Nietzschean "event" in *The Shortest Shadow*, 11.
4 Zupančič, *The Shortest Shadow*, 8.
5 Friedrich Nietzsche, *The Twilight of the Idols* (Penguin, 1990), 51. Cited in *The Shortest Shadow*, 27.
6 Zupančič, *The Shortest Shadow*, 6.
7 Zupančič, 8.
8 Zupančič, 35.
9 Zupančič writes, "Why bother with knowledge, if we 'know' that—to put it as simply as possible—this is not the way to happiness, that it cannot promise any final redemption or salvation? In other words, the very passion for knowledge and truth appears here as *meaningless*. This, of course, is one of the definitions of nihilism," *The Shortest Shadow*, 153.
10 Zupančič, 38.
11 Max Weber, *The Protestant Ethic and the Spirit of Capitalism* (Roxbury Publishing, 2002).
12 Zupančič, *The Shortest Shadow*, 38.
13 Zupančič speaks of anorexia in this regard in *The Shortest Shadow*, 128–9.
14 Zupančič, *The Shortest Shadow*, 125.
15 Jacques Lacan, *Seminar XI: The Four Fundamentals of Psycho-Analysis* (Routledge, 2018), 211.
16 Slavoj Žižek, *Did Somebody Say Totalitarianism? Five Interventions in the (Mis)use of a Notion* (Verso, 2001), 240.
17 Slavoj Žižek, "Clinton, Trump and the Left's Dilemma," *In These Times*, 6 November 2016, https://inthesetimes.com/features/zizek_clinton_trump_lesser_evil.html.
18 Zupančič, *The Shortest Shadow*, 138.
19 Zupančič writes, "The way Nietzsche solves this problem is not by adding, as a third term to the dichotomy of Yes and No, something like 'perhaps,' or 'neither Yes nor No'—he adds another Yes, another affirmation," *The Shortest Shadow*, 134. This is not unrelated to Nietzsche's thinking of the contingency of necessity. See on this *The Shortest Shadow*, 161–2. Notably, Derrida throughout his work also insists on this doubled or repeated "Yes," this "Yes" to a "Yes." See, for example, "Ulysses Gramophone: Hear Say Yes in Joyce," in *Acts of Literature* (Routledge, 1992).
20 Zupančič, *The Shortest Shadow*, 25.
21 Zupančič, 172. In fact, we could say that what we are speaking of here is both an "object of experience" and the "thing in itself."
22 On the inseparability of sublimation and desublimation, see *The Shortest Shadow*, 179–80.
23 Zupančič writes on the impossibility of an overall perspective and the way the only true perspective is "in the middle" in *The Shortest Shadow*, 97–99.

24 Jacques Derrida, "Of an Apocalyptic Tone Recently Adopted in Philosophy," *Oxford Literary Review* 6, no. 2 (1984): 3–37.

25 Jacques Derrida, "Structure, Sign and Play in the Discourse of the Human Sciences," in *Writing and Difference* (Routledge, 2001), 354. See also Alain Badiou's obituary for Derrida: "He was brave because it takes a lot of courage not to enter into the division as it was constituted . . . For any true peace is based upon an agreement not about that which exists, but about that which non-exists . . . This diagonal obstinacy, this rejection of abrupt metaphysically derived divisions, is obviously not suited to stormy times when everything comes under the law of decisiveness, here and now . . . Because the truth of those years spoke its name with the words 'One divides into two,'" *Pocket Pantheon: Figures of Postwar Philosophy* (Verso, 2016), 137–8.

26 See, for example, where Zupančič speaks of Deleuze's account of Nietzsche in terms of "disjunctive synthesis" and "conjunctive analysis," which would be exactly that kind of "self-splitting" she is trying to elaborate, in *The Shortest Shadow*, 87.

27 Gilles Deleuze and Félix Guattari, *A Thousand Plateaus: Capitalism and Schizophrenia* (University of Minneapolis Press, 1987), 10.

28 Jean Baudrillard, *Fragments: Conversations with François L'Yvonnet* (Routledge, 2004), 1.

29 Jean Baudrillard, *In the Shadow of the Silent Majorities* (Semiotext(e), 2007), 38.

30 Or Lyotard can be seen to be suggesting that we already have this "putting together" of the Idea and its object in Kant. See on this his *Lessons on the Analytic of the Sublime: Kant's Critique of Judgement, 23–29* (Meridian, 1994): "The object that is presented to reason in the phenomenon is never 'big enough' with respect to the object of its Idea, and for the imagination the latter is always 'too big' to be presentable. The differend cannot be resolved. But it can be felt as such, as differend. This is the sublime feeling" (233–4).

31 Jean-François Lyotard, *The Postmodern Condition: A Report on Knowledge* (University of Minnesota Press, 1984), 81.

32 Zupančič, *The Shortest Shadow*, 163.

Dionysos in the Antipodes: Nietzsche, Norman and Jack Lindsay, Bernard Smith

Ian McLean

Dionysos in the Antipodes

The obvious place to start with a discussion of Nietzsche's footprint in the Australian art world is Norman Lindsay (1879–1969). A renowned Australian cartoonist, artist, and writer during the first four decades of the twentieth century, Lindsay made no secret of his Nietzscheanism as a cure for the world's ills, in which he included modernism, Christianity, the British mindset, and their empires and values. In the early 1920s, the intensifying whirlwinds of the new century would draw Norman's son Jack Lindsay (1900–90) into his father's Nietzschean enclave, inspiring him to write *Dionysos: Nietzsche contra Nietzsche: An Essay in Lyrical Philosophy* (1928). Although the efforts of this father–son duo are overlooked today in the broader landscape of Australian art history and modernism, the two captured the attention of Australia's preeminent art historian of the twentieth century, Bernard Smith (1916–2011). Despite the historian's life-long aversion to Nietzschean philosophy, Smith's Marxism was, like that of Jack's, intensely interested in the moral questions asked by Nietzsche and their implications for art. The programmatic nature of the Lindsays' and Smith's vision makes the story of this trio the most encompassing account of Nietzsche's legacy in Australian art, though it only touches a few examples of its antipodean reach.

Smith's two main publications on Australian art, *Australian Painting* (1962) and his first book *Place, Taste and Tradition: A Study of Australian Art Since 1788* (1945), make only a few fleeting references to Nietzsche. This is also the case with his last major book, the ambitious *Modernism's History* (1998), into which he poured his life's learning. But if Smith has little to say about Nietzsche, he blames him for everything that went wrong with the twentieth century, from the formalism, primitivism, and spiritualism of modernist abstraction to the First World War, Nazism, and what he considered the blight of Lindsay and his art. Forever suspicious of Nietzsche's elitism, Smith wrote of Nietzsche in 1975 that he was "a god to himself," "a man beyond morality who listens to his inner voice, which is no longer the voice of conscience but a primitive creative daemon."[1] As for Lindsay, Smith was adamant, writing in 1976, that he "was not a genius," as he was often called in his day, and "lacked originality of mind."[2]

Yet Smith regarded Lindsay's son Jack as "one of the most original thinkers of the present century," coming under his influence in 1939 when he acquired and heavily annotated his book *A Short History of Culture*.[3] Despite the Nietzschean undercurrent in Jack's thinking, and attracted by his Marxism and extensive writings on art and culture, Smith found in Jack a valued mentor.

1901: Birth of an Idea

Few noticed, but the idea of an Australian art took breath at the dawn of the twentieth century in Sydney, Australia. On 1 January 1901, at a crowded ceremony full of the pomp of Empire and English entitlement, the British Crown dissolved the separate administration of its self-governing Australian colonies, proclaiming them reborn as states unified in a federated Commonwealth of Australia. The promise of a postcolonial national culture beckoned. On that day, Lindsay was a twenty-one-year-old struggling artist living in Melbourne, and father of two-month-old Jack. Smith's birth was fifteen years away, by which time Lindsay was being hailed by Australian critics and the public as a living genius, and Nietzsche's name was on everyone's lips.

On 1 January 1901, Nietzsche was dead, four months buried in the family plot in Weimar, Germany. But his ghost was stirring. In 1901, his estate published *The Will to Power*, which comprised nearly five hundred aphorisms taken from his notebooks of 1883–88. The definitive 1906 edition would contain more than one thousand aphorisms. As though Nietzsche was speaking from the afterlife, the preface made a call to arms that would galvanise the new generations:

> I describe what is coming, what can no longer come differently: *the advent of nihilism* . . . this destiny announces itself everywhere . . . our whole European culture has been moving as toward a catastrophe . . . restlessly, violently, headlong . . . make no mistake about the meaning of the title that this gospel of the future wants to bear. "*The Will to Power*: Attempt at a Revaluation of All Values."

Each generation is tasked with navigating the destiny it inherits. Nietzsche felt the force of a new cosmology propagated by the likes of Charles Darwin, Karl Marx, and Frederick Engels. Drawing from the latest research on the origins of life and mankind, their radical tracts challenged the idea of God as the transcendent origin of all things. In the twentieth century, Nietzsche would join this posse of Antichrists. Their revolutionary ideas tore through humanity in the upheavals of the twentieth century as the world's empires imploded. Touching a nerve in the collective psyche of those who came of age during this first apocalyptic half of the century, Nietzsche became a cult figure. The "strongest effects," Nietzsche wrote, are produced "in ages when tragedy walks abroad."[4] He should know, for he was tragedy walking abroad: his books unnoticed, his health in ruins, his catastrophic collapse on the third day of 1889 while intervening, the story goes, in the whipping of a horse. It left him delusional, uncommunicative, and finally silent.

Virtually ignored in his lifetime, all those words that had poured forth in his furious final decade of writing unleashed their energy on the new twentieth century. His very name had an afterlife that wielded the power of myth as a brand. You didn't need to read his books to imbibe his sermons. Many began to feel their feelings in his, making his aphorisms an alibi for every new creed: modernists, antimodernists, and postmodernists; theosophists, eugenicists, and vitalists; communists, capitalists, fascists, anarchists, hippies, New-Ageists, neo-liberals, neo-Nazis, and, despite Nietzsche's notorious misogyny, even feminists. It wasn't so much what he said, but that his spirited style resonated with the unsettled zeitgeist of the day. It intoxicated Lindsay when he first read *Zarathustra* at the close of the nineteenth century:

> The exaltation I was given by that inspired work transfigured for me all profundities in life and art. One does not merely read such works . . . The passion inspired by them is absorbed into the very substance of the ego.[5]

What had Nietzsche preached that in the late 1890s cast such a spell on Lindsay, and some twenty years later on his son?

The Spell of Antipodal Logic: Nietzsche contra Nietzsche

Positive and negative. – This thinker needs no one to refute him: he does that for himself. (*The Wanderer and His Shadow*, 249, 1880)

In one's friend one should have one's best enemy. ("The friend," *Thus Spoke Zarathustra*, 1883)

Not until all of you have disowned me shall I return unto you. ("Of Giving Virtue," *Thus Spoke Zarathustra*, 1883)

Truth is ugly. We possess art lest we perish of the truth. (*The Will to Power,* 822, 1888)

"Dionysian" means the feeling of the necessary unity of creation and destruction. (*The Will to Power*, 1050, 1888)

We are antipodes. ("Preface," *Nietzsche contra Wagner*, 1888)

Thus spoke Nietzsche in an ironic, performative rhetoric that courted inversion and contradiction. He published thousands of such aphorisms in about a dozen books written between 1878 and 1888, generally in numbered paragraphs ranging from a sentence or two to a page or more. Many are commentaries on his first book, *The Birth of Tragedy* (1872). Beholden to neither the "falsifying" deductive logic in which he had been trained as an academic nor the inferences of common-sense empiricism,[6] Nietzsche honed the sharper tongue and emotional charge of polemic and aphorism that is the consort of poetry. To his precocious would-be student and first biographer Lou Salomé, he advised "stepping close to poetry but never stepping in it . . . one must *learn* to feel everything: 'The more abstract a truth one wishes to teach, the more one must seduce the *senses*.'" "The prime necessity," he emphasised, "is life; a style should *live* . . . Style ought to prove that one *believes* in an idea; not only thinks it but also feels it."[7]

Nietzsche's driving motive was the total and so radical "revaluation of all values." While Europe's empires had never been so wealthy and powerful, they appeared to Nietzsche spiritually bankrupt. Their epistemologies unable to navigate a labile modernity, Nietzsche prescribed an emotionally embodied thinking that required an appropriately fugitive language. Hence, despite his predisposition for clarity, Nietzsche's phrasing, said his leading English translator Walter Kaufmann, is crafted to convey "a double meaning": he "loved language as poets do," especially "words and phrases that mean one thing out of context and almost the opposite in the context he gives them."[8] This returned language to its primal origin in the inherent relationality of its representational function as symbol, effectively recreating what it represents. "What *things are called*," said Nietzsche, "is unspeakably more important than what they are . . . what started as appearance in the end nearly always becomes essence and effectively acts as its essence!"[9]

In doubling what it represents, language is an ambivalent binary construct open to antipodal manoeuvres. Each of the above-cited epigraphs hit the spot by inverting conventional values through the ironic play of language—"the knack," said Nietzsche, "of reversing perspectives: the first reason . . . why a Transvaluation of all Values has been possible."[10] If language creates a virtual world that overdetermines what it represents, Nietzsche, perhaps jokingly, proposed a natural basis of his innate contrariness in the double origin of his conception—the noble Polish ancestry of his father and the "diametric opposite . . . shabby" ancestry of his German mother.[11] It finds, he said,

> in every detail its counterpart in my own nature—I am my own complement . . . I was allowed an outlook beyond all merely local, merely national and limited horizons; it required no effort on my part to be a "good European."[12]

Nietzsche felt the torque of antipodal logic as a psychological disposition. "He observed himself as his double," argued Salomé, which he called variously his "shadow" and "dwarf."

He encountered them when he walked mountain-goat paths alone in a bid to reconnect with life / nature. This was how, said Nietzsche, "all Zarathustra came to me, above all, Zarathustra himself as a type."[13] These weren't convivial encounters; rather, his shadow taunted him as if an uncanny double, a demon. "'There is always one too many about me,'" said Zarathustra, "'I and me are always too eager in a conversation: how could it be borne if there were not a friend?'" Then, in typical antipodal fashion, Nietzsche twists the knife: "Our longing for a friend is our betrayer," a "third one" which diminishes the double's daemonic Dionysian energy that arises within, especially at moments of crisis.[14]

Nietzsche dubbed the extraordinary yield of his last fevered decade of writing "the memorial of a crisis." It followed a series of personal upheavals that began in the latter half of the 1870s: debilitating migraines, failing eyesight, his fraught break with Wagner in 1876, termination of his university career, rejected marriage proposals (Salomé was his great disappointment), and infuriation with his meddling mother and sister. The perennial optimist, Nietzsche counted these destructive traumas as creative blessings "to reverse my mode of life . . . Never have I rejoiced more over my condition than during the sickest and most painful moments of my life."[15]

Nietzsche's doubleness pre-empts the irreducible split subject theorised by psychoanalysis: "Unto thy side I jumped. Then thou fleddest back from my bound. And towards me played the tongue of thy hair fleeing, flying round!"[16] This uncanny taunting of the double, imagined here as a Siren (possibly based on Salomé), is the haunting of a lost whole that can't be redeemed. Imagining that it can be redeemed by negating one side of its binary, said Nietzsche, is the "*holy lie*" of ideology.[17] He specifically had religion in his sights, but also nationalism, anti-Semitism, and feminism. Nor could the binary terms of the split subject be overcome through a dialectical synthesis to a higher ideal, a "third one." It wasn't a matter of choosing between or overcoming one's split doubleness, but of appreciating its eternal contrapposto turns in which "the essential duality of all energy is simultaneously reconciled and vitalised into deeper discord"—as Jack, one of Nietzsche's disciples, put it in *Dionysos: Nietzsche contra Nietzsche* (1928).[18]

Coming under Nietzsche's spell via his father, Jack's unpublished autobiography (1970) began by announcing his inheritance of Nietzsche's Dionysian spirit, as if Nietzsche had been reborn in the Antipodes, in him, Jack Lindsay: "I was born in October 1900, in Melbourne, Australia. That year Nietzsche died."[19]

Jack had first recognised Nietzsche's spirit moving in him "from a day in 1919 when I took an oath of total resistance to the world about me." His alienation had been building for a decade, beginning in 1909 when his father abandoned the family. It intensified during his teenage years in Brisbane with his discovery of literature—the Greek myths, Shakespeare, Blake, Dostoevsky, and Sassoon's war poems. Read against the crushing events of the First World War, Jack felt "the betrayal of human brotherhood": "The murder was everywhere, the gutters ran with blood. Every human relationship was perverse and corrupt if it did not hold at its core the revolt against the reigning inhumanity."[20]

His spirit began to lift with the Russian Revolution in 1917 and the seduction of socialism, but his resolve of "total resistance" was triggered by reconciliation with his father in 1919, who had sent him a copy of *Zarathustra*, some examples of his art, and the proof copy of his book *Creative Effort*. Unlike his father, for Jack, reading Nietzsche was more a social than personal revelation: "I saw that I also was within history, participating whether I liked it or not. I read a newspaper, and the voice read it for me, the stormy voice revaluing all values."[21] This "stormvoice" would open the door to Marxism, in which he heard "all the voices in history":

> The inner conflict of values, fought out in George Street and the upper reaches of the Brisbane River, was found to be identical with a conflict which had been going on for quite a long time in history . . . But Nietzsche . . . added something central by his unfaltering emphasis on the moral issue of creative renewal, the eternal-recurrence of Dionysos.[22]

Jack never repudiated Nietzsche, but his publication of *The Anatomy of Spirit* (1937) and *A Short History of Culture* (1939) broke from his father's elitist sense of being a chosen one of the Olympian gods. Instead, applying Marxism's "dialectical materialism" to a "social-economic approach" and the latest research in archaeology and anthropology, Jack traced the development of spirit or culture throughout human history.[23] Anticipating structuralism, he elevated Nietzsche's antipodal logic to a universal principle that determined the "basic structural lines of culture."[24] It was first fully evident, said Jack, in the doubled cosmology of totemism, which imagined the individual inhabiting a parallel spirit world to the physical world, the "individual double." Like a persistent "rhythm," he said, this sense of doubleness, of being both embodied and possessing a spirit form, appears in all cultures: "The Roman thought he had a *genius*, and the Greek thought he had a *daimon*."[25]

Nietzsche is barely mentioned by name in these two books, but his antipodal logic echoes throughout, as if he was reborn in Marxist guise. Because "we find the way forward through what destroys us," said Jack, "for the socialist writer the problem is to grasp this conflict . . . and its resolution."[26] He believed his father had done this at the turn of the century in his early drawings of Dionysian revolt beneath eucalyptus trees. With them, "Australian culture entered on a new phase . . . [that] proclaimed the death of all provincialism" and demanded "Australia enter the currents of world-culture." They pointed, said Jack, to how "the nation [could] leap from the bush-ballad" and the "feeble imitation of the superficial aspects" of European culture to an art "adequate to the modern world."[27]

The first such drawing to attract public attention, the large pen-and-ink *Pollice verso*, depicts a cavorting crowd of naked athletic women and men jeering at an emaciated Christ on the cross. Made and exhibited in 1904, it launched Lindsay's career, fuelled by the outcry of the moral police. Much to their alarm, other drawings from this time such as *The Scoffers* (1903), *The Vintage Festival* (1905), and *The Picnic God* (1907) celebrated the sexual energy of Australian Amazonians and satyrs upturning British Victorian values. The only explanation for the attitude of "these gentle feeble darlings,—the cultured mob," said Lindsay in 1904, is "the real moral instinct of my work." Brazenly channelling Nietzsche in a letter to Australia's most popular weekly newspaper, the Left-leaning republican *Bulletin*, where he was its star cartoonist, he made his case:

> It is simply a statement of my belief in animal force, the right of the healthy and the strong over the weak and the ill constituted, the Saturnalia that is a part of all ascending life . . . All those qualities the ancient world understood as simple matters. because it believed unquestionably in its instincts, but which the modern mind, hedged about with half-truths and sentimentalities, instinctively knows to be its enemies.[28]

Creative Effort

The First World War shook Lindsay to the core, as it did many, creating a post-war saturnine zeitgeist that made Oswald Spengler's *Decline of the West* (1918) a bestseller. It galvanised Lindsay to write *Creative Effort* (1920), and to embark on a mission to save the world by making Australia, as Smith put it, "the centre of a new white civilisation . . . freed from the injustices of old Europe."[29] The Lindsay circle, which included Jack, advanced their cause in Sydney's short-lived quarterly magazine *Vision*:

> Considering the depths of devitalisation the world touched in the War . . . it is clear that unless consciousness soon takes an upward turn, vitality will sink too low ever to recover. A Renaissance is a necessity, and we believe that already the stirring of the wings can be felt . . . If Australia alone in the world is doing this—and we see no evidence for any other conclusion—then the Renaissance must begin from here.

Smith argued that Nietzsche's dismissal of contemporary European civilisation inspired modernism's anachronistic consciousness that looked for inspiration in "archaistic" European art, such as classical Greece and Rome and "primitivistic" exotic cultures in Africa and Oceania.[30] Anachronism's untimeliness, Nietzsche wrote, "returns as a ghost and disturbs the peace of a later moment,"[31] thereby creating a historical consciousness with which to "combat our inborn heritage and implant in ourselves a new habit, a new instinct, a second nature, so that our first nature withers away." In this way, one acquires "a past in which one would like to originate in opposition to that in which one did originate."[32] Such was the hope of *Vision,* which broadcast a call for a Nietzschean poetics "that liberates imagination by gaiety or fantasy," its symbol the faun, its "roots deep in life and sensation . . . who cries the songs of Olympos amid the woods of the earth," as Dionysos did.[33] Like the original "Culture-Hero" of "totemist days," wrote Jack, they embodied the "harmony [with nature] imaged in the totem animal or plant," making them "twin culture heroes," the first artists, the makers of doubles.[34] With their creative powers descended from the Olympian immortals, artists and poets are proclaimed by Lindsay as "the aristocrats of the Future."[35] "Least of all to be considered," he said, "are those feminine half-minds that find in creeds, political or religious, a direction for life."[36]

In the Nietzschean creed, said Salomé, "the highest ethical work is only *a work of art,*" such that "ethics unobtrusively merges with aesthetics—into a kind of religious aesthetics . . . the divinity of the beautiful."[37] Art affirms life, said Nietzsche, because the suffering and tragedy of "existence . . . is justified only as an aesthetic phenomenon,"[38] making "art . . . the highest task and the properly metaphysical activity of this life."[39] Thus, Nietzsche wrote:

> I agree more with the artists than with any philosopher hitherto; they have not lost the scent of life, they have loved the things of "this world"—they have loved their senses. To strive for "desensualization": that seems to me a misunderstanding . . . we should be grateful to the senses

> for their subtlety, plenitude, and power and offer them in return the best we have in the way of spirit.[40]

Nietzsche and Lindsay each put their faith in the artist, but they diverged on the detail. The war had shattered Lindsay's faith in the power of the senses. The "gift of earth to man" is the "five senses, and the function of Sex," whereas *Creative Effort* demanded "the development of mind [which] goes on by quite another process . . . beyond the primitive stimulus of the senses."[41] His search for this imaginative realm beyond the body's senses is evident in the shift from the earthy realism of his earlier work to the formulaic idealism of his post-war compositions.

In the escalating degeneracy of post-war Europe, Lindsay's conundrum was ensuring the mind's sovereignty when the intellect requires "the senses which obstruct the [creative] effort."[42] The sexual energy of his Amazonian muses often took an increasingly spiritualised demeanour, from the beatific and ethereal fantasias of *Virginity* (1921) and *Adolescence* (1923), to the daemonic *Enter the Magicians* (1927) and *Self-Portrait* (1930).[43] Was this a mirror to the tragedy then stalking the world, as if the only way forward for Lindsay was to strategically retreat from the world of earthly delights, as Zarathustra had done? Jack thought so:

> The shock which the war gave him has . . . abstracted Art and Spirit into an autonomous sphere unrelated to earthly process, a sort of Gnosticism retaining Nietzsche's lonely defiance but not his acclamation of the earth.[44]

Lindsay envisaged this "transcendental revenge"—as Jack dubbed his father's post-war turn[45]—as a strategic regrouping to prepare for the coming of a new cultural hero equipped with the "imagination . . . to see beyond the actual thing to its imaginative analogy in a higher condition of sense."[46] Only such a "strong vitality of mind," said Lindsay, could "startle consciousness back to the real problems of life, which are those of passion and beauty; but, most of all, Sex":

> he . . . will be the lover as well as one who sings of love. Women will no longer be little overdressed shadows of a sociological problem, but will return to our embrace naked and lovely, offering their plump hands with long tapering fingers, and their white breasts to our devout kisses. We will wed this proud femininity to our dreams, . . . Once again Love will be adorable . . . the spirit that takes its flight upward will not sing of Heaven, but of the living beauty of "Flesh clasped naked in a web of pearls."[47]

The Mask of Art and the Gender of Truth

While Nietzsche and Lindsay each regarded art and philosophy as twin practices, Nietzsche focused on the role of art in his philosophical scheme, whereas Lindsay aimed to give his art a philosophical justification. Both admired the classical tragic genre, though Lindsay's taste inclined strongly to its antipodes in Rabelais. If Lindsay's is an art of ribald fantasy and pantomime, Nietzsche exhibits a stately classical sense of restraint and decorum. He lauds the Dionysian underbelly of the tragic mode only if it ruffles, without removing, the decorous Apollonian "veil" of beauty that conceals the horrific truths of nature. His sensibility tends to the antipodal structure of the sublime, which desires a tantalising glimpse of, but protective screen from, truth's horror.[48] This is what, for Nietzsche, makes art "*worth more* than truth."[49] Like artists, he said, we must learn to "be good at not knowing! . . . to stop bravely at the surface, the fold, the skin; to worship appearance, to believe in shapes, tones, words—in the whole Olympus of appearance!"[50]

Given Nietzsche's habit of finding solace on mountain paths, the anti-naturalism of his example is revealing of what revealing does, which is re-veiling: "when we love a woman, we easily come to hate nature because of all the repulsive natural functions to which every woman is subject." Hence, he opined, "We artists . . . conceal what is natural,"[51] and commended "the very desirable veil over a pudendum":[52]

> We no longer believe that truth remains truth when the veils are withdrawn. Today we consider it a matter of decency not to wish to see everything naked, to be present at everything, to understand and "know" everything.[53]

Hence, Nietzsche was not disposed to Lindsay's obsession with the female nude and was incredulous at the Kantian proposition "that, under the spell of beauty, one can even view undraped female statues 'without interest.'"[54] Unlike Lindsay, Nietzsche idealised the artist as a celibate genius who practised "a relative chastity . . . even in thought." Not only is the artist especially "susceptible in every sense to stimuli" but also "the force that one expends in artistic conception is the same as that expended in the sexual act." "An artist," Nietzsche wrote, "betrays himself if he succumbs here . . . it can be a sign of decadence."[55]

Such prudery is in keeping with Nietzsche's notorious misogyny, or so thought Jack. He blamed it on the "sexual fear" of this "chaste man," epitomised, said Jack, in the infamous aphorism of *Zarathustra*: "Goest thou to woman? Forget not thy whip."[56] Nietzsche's disdain for women pockmarks his writing. Believing women were "'more natural' than . . . men," he warned against their "truly predatory and cunning agility . . . their inner wildness and inability to be trained."[57] Few things riled him more than talk of women's emancipation. No doubt he was thinking of the "pseudo-girl" Salomé when he wrote: "when a woman has scholarly leanings, usually something is out of order with her sexually."[58]

But then there is the antipodal rip current of Nietzsche's thinking. Jacques Derrida, whose deconstructions gave truth a good whipping, read Nietzsche's "venomous anti-feminism" antipodally or against its grain.[59] So too have several other poststructuralists, including some associated with feminism.[60] Nietzsche wrote that women, being "at best, cows,"[61] have no need of self-overcoming, because, being at home in their animality, they are already truth triumphant: "Truth is a woman," said Nietzsche, because she understands truth as subjective, elusive, and performative, a fiction.[62] "What does truth matter for a woman! . . . their great art is in lying, their highest concern is appearance and beauty," making them natural artists.[63] "Indeed," he exclaimed thrice, "our artists are painfully like hysterical females!!!"[64] And so too, said Derrida, is Nietzsche: he "writes with the hand of woman."[65]

For Nietzsche, the artist, not the philosopher, is the higher man or Übermensch, because she does not want truth. As if intuitively understanding this, Lindsay depicted the higher man in the likeness of his muse, lover, and antichrist, Rose Lindsay (née Soady). In *Vision*, she appeared in fanciful vignettes as the antipodean Dionysos. Having parted ways on the detail, Nietzsche and Lindsay meet again on the gender of truth.

Dionysos in the Antipodes: Bernard Smith

Smith had as little patience for Derrida's "*obscurantisme terroristé*" as he did for Lindsay's fantasies and Nietzsche's antipodal logic.[66] That "'we must destroy . . . before we can go forward,'" wrote Smith in 1983, "was an attitude that I profoundly distrusted."[67] He also dismissed the spiritual speculations of theosophy and "other modernist religions" that were influential on Lindsay and their joint bête noire, the abstractionists.[68] In 1976, on the eve of his retirement, Smith satirised Lindsay's Nietzschean credo as "the noble frontiersman seeks redemption by ritual acts of love and sex upon the white mother-goddess of Austra-lo-European nature," dismissing as delusional his "antisemitism, his spiritualism, his belief in the existence of Atlantis," and his "rejection of all forms of modernism as cultural degeneration."[69]

Smith even blamed Nietzsche for "the white blanket of forgetfulness [thrown] across the central tragedy of Australian settlement," which the Impressionists fashioned as a (Nietzschean) veil of art depicting the "pastoralist dream of a sun-kissed Arcadia."[70] The accusation appeared in his impassioned 1980 Boyer Lectures broadcast on national radio. A damning indictment of Australian colonial practices, Smith argued that its art worked "to blot from their memories the crimes perpetrated upon Australia's first inhabitants."[71] This was the pot calling the kettle black.

The Boyer Lectures blew the lid off a history of Australian art in which Smith was complicit, but it took another twenty years for Smith to confess: "during my professional career I had said virtually nothing about Aboriginal art."[72] In practising the same "mechanisms of forgetfulness" that he ascribed to the influence of Nietzsche,[73] Smith implicitly admits his own Nietzschean descent.

Smith was in no mood to redeem either Nietzsche nor Lindsay, but he had become intrigued by the mission of Jack to free Australians from their colonial fate and make them a cultural force in the world. Recalling their time in the 1920s, when Europe was "culturally exhausted, going down into a swamp of primitivism, a desert of abstraction," it seemed to them, wrote Jack, that its antipodes, Australia, was well placed to expediate the revaluation of all values.[74] Intuiting in Nietzsche "something that European thinkers did not find,"[75]

> we sought to refound the [classical] Grand Tradition . . . on Australian soil. We rejected "nationalism" in art because we identified it with parochialism . . . so denying our Australian links, we proclaimed an Australian Renaissance. Zarathustra announced himself in Springwood. We saw that, but we failed to note his Australian accent.[76]

Jack continued the campaign when he moved permanently to London in 1926. In 1983, Smith characterised it as a "vigorous attempt to weld together creative dissident elements, Irish, Welsh, South African as well as Australian, that were opposed to modernism" and British imperialism.[77] "In retrospect," continued Smith, "the whole idea may sound laughable . . . but there was nothing historically absurd in the proposal that the values of the fringe, the edge, the province, might overturn the values of the centre."[78]

These sentiments were already evident in two of Smith's most cited texts, *Antipodean Manifesto* (1959) and *European Vision and the South Pacific* (1960). Of the latter, now widely seen as a premonition of postcolonial criticism, Peter Beilharz wrote, "Smith refuses the idea that culture like power flows unilaterally, from the centre out onto the peripheries. Smith is more interested in how different cultures converge . . . become entangled."[79] This is also true of the *Antipodean Manifesto*. For Smith, Beilharz explained, "The antipodes is not a place so much as it is a relation . . . [which] enables us,"[80] and nothing had pleased Smith more than the name being quickly "grabbed . . . to define a whole trend in Australian art."[81]

Militant in tone, it was envisaged as a strike against the latest modernist abstraction emanating from the centre by art with an Australian accent "of vitality and power . . . something which is vital to the life of art itself." Eschewing the parochialism of nationalism and arguing for "the independent creative activity of the artist," the *Antipodean Manifesto* committed to a contemporary art involved "in life . . . whether of the flesh or of the spirit."[82] Even if unconscious, such phrasing suggests that Smith had been reading the Lindsays and even Nietzsche—most likely Golffing's 1956 translation of *The Birth of Tragedy* and *The Genealogy of Morals*, which Smith owned and had heavily annotated. Yet no one, not even Smith, seemed to notice the Nietzschean undercurrents of the *Antipodean Manifesto* and its vision of an antipodean redemption.

In the mid-twentieth century, the Nazi celebration of Nietzsche cast a veil over his legacy. For Smith, this veil was woven into the fabric of his anti-fascism forged by his communist commitments in the late 1930s and 1940s.[83] Hence, the only reference to Nietzsche in Smith's main publication of the war years, *Place, Taste and Tradition*—written, he said, as his contribution to the war against fascism[84]—was damning. Nietzsche was condemned as midwife to the esoteric otherworldly spiritualism and aestheticism of abstract art and "the flight from reason, of which Fascism was the most vicious consummation."[85] Smith didn't mention Lindsay's Nietzscheanism, despite it being public knowledge, though his description of Lindsay as "the high priest of aestheticism in Australia" said as much.[86] Smith evidently felt his case for the anachronisms of Norman's "ersatz rococo variations" was better made by comparing him to the English Decadents Aubrey Beardsley and Oscar Wilde.[87] "A rebel of the boudoir"[88] was Smith's cutting verdict: Lindsay's "little pre-Disney fantasies to amuse an antipodean cult endeavouring to be international" belong "to the pseudo-pastoralism of Marie Antionette, and . . . the vistas of Versailles," not the real world.[89]

When a second edition of *Place, Taste and Tradition* was published in 1979, Smith found virtually nothing to change,[90] even though *Australian Painting* (1962) had been more generous to Lindsay:

> During the first two decades of the present [twentieth] century, Norman Lindsay was the most controversial figure in Australian art and letters . . . the most talented, imaginative and prolific pen draughtsman in the country, and the effect of his work and thought extended eventually to the whole field of Australian culture . . . [becoming] a liberating force of considerable power."[91]

Yet in the same breath, Smith judged that Nietzsche's "influence upon Australian painting has been of no great significance," as if not noticing the contradiction. Smith's initial idea that a national tradition of Australian art had developed in resistance to classicism had not changed. Identifying classicism as a style of European imperialism, its impact, he said, resulted in "an 'unAustralian' portrayal" of Australian subjects, especially evident in the colonists' depictions of Aboriginal Australians. He also claimed that classicism was Western art's first primitivism because it idealised an ancestral past.[92] He pointed to its echoes in the primitivism of fascist and modernist tendencies, as in the art of Australian painter and printmaker Margaret Preston (1875–1963), in which "the aboriginal" was endowed "by latter-day Australian nationalism as the role of 'racial father' to the descendants of a West-European nation." Smith's simultaneous categorical exclusion of Aboriginal art from the idea of Australian art can also be seen in this light.[93]

Smith's retirement in 1977 seemingly initiated a reassessment of these earlier attitudes, in which, over the next decade, classicism, primitivism, Nietzsche, Lindsay, Preston, and Aboriginal art were positively revalued. In his collection of theoretical essays *The Death of the Artist as Hero: Essays in History and Culture* (1988)—most of which were written after the 1960s—the three most frequently referenced persons are Marx and Norman and Jack Lindsay. Nietzsche also features prominently, reflecting that five out of the six titles Smith owned by Nietzsche were editions published between 1973 and 1979. The most likely reason for this sudden interest in Nietzsche is Smith's preparation for his edited book *Culture and History: Essays presented to Jack Lindsay* (1984). As becomes increasingly apparent in Smith's subsequent writing, befriending Jack in the late 1940s while studying in London precipitated a slow-burning reassessment of not just Nietzsche and Lindsay, but also their joint passion for classicism.

In 1984, in his article "Is There a Radical Tradition in Australian Art?," Smith made classicism and primitivism essential ingredients in what he dubbed "a radical tradition in Australian art." Sharpening his long-held belief that Aboriginal art was the only "*art-form* peculiar to this continent," and choosing his terminology carefully, he distinguished between this truly "Australian art" and "art in Australia," by which he meant the importation of European styles "in its colonial and post-colonial manifestations." In the latter, he identified a "radical tradition" that, since the beginning of the twentieth century, has been "steadily transforming art in Australia into Australian art."[94] He was primarily concerned with distinguishing it from artists he called the "innovators," whose importation of modernism's ongoing innovation, he wrote, is "more often than not the principal way in which conservative traditions maintain their oppressive power."[95] In thrall of European models, the "innovators" are the "most influential opponents of an independent and radical art in Australia,"[96] whereas "the radical," said Smith in a Nietzschean accent, "seeks change . . . of a substantial nature" by invoking "an image of a finer past," such that "some kind of classicism or the primitive seems to be present in all radical ideology."[97]

The innovators had a style around which they rallied, namely European modernism, but the radicals shared no identifiable style. "It was a discontinuous tradition," said Smith, "not a family affair," but it shared a historical consciousness that had a "firm national component."[98] He suggested with some qualification that the first radicals were the Impressionists Tom Roberts and Fred McCubbin, as they "turned back to colonial history." He was more emphatic that Preston and Lindsay were important radicals, despite having previously associated them with the fascist mentality in Australian art. The "radical aspect" of Preston's work, he said, was its "primitivism," whereas, against "the puritanical moral institutions of colonial culture . . . and their source in British culture," Lindsay opposed "a liberating sexuality . . . based on [classical] Greek models." Further, Smith added, "in the 1920s his aggressive radicalism had taken the form of a vision . . . of an Australian renascence of Europe's declining culture"[99]—as if Lindsay was a proto-Antipodean.

An unusual example of Smith's late appreciation of classicism is his portrait entered in the nation's most anticipated art event, the Archibald portrait prize. In 2002, after reading Smith's *Antipodean Manifesto* (1959), the artist Carmel O'Connor approached the art historian to sit for a portrait. Smith agreed on condition that he appeared nude as the *Barberini Faun*, as if he secretly or unconsciously wished to feature in a Lindsay-like composition as an anachronistic Antipodean Dionysos.[100] The reason Smith gave is that "I want to get away from being put into a respectable box," which is another way of claiming his radicality.[101]

The radicals that most excited Smith were the small group of artists of his generation who identified with European avant-garde art of the 1920s and '30s: the Angry Penguins, Social Realists, and his own Surrealist paintings. His paintings, he said, were in 1940 "far too radical even for the political left to accept."[102] While this generation practised, Smith said, "a radicalism of modernism," it was also a "critique of modernism" that in Australia "begins with Lindsay."[103] In the second updated edition of *Australian Painting* published in 1971, Smith had also singled out the Melbourne-based artist Leonard French (1927–2017) as "one of the most highly original and creative talents" of the 1960s. Arguing for his "affinity with Nietzsche," he praised French's treatment of the universal mythic "hero"—"Greek and Dionysiac Greek at that, in Nietzsche's sense."[104]

In the 1980s, Smith had found a way to redeem classicism, primitivism, Nietzsche, Lindsay, and Preston, each of which he had argued against as forces of un-Australian art. This would not be the case with Aboriginal art, even though he also gained a new appreciation of it at the same time. Smith's inclusion of Preston in the select pantheon of radical Australian art coincided with his own conversion to her transcultural aesthetic. From 1980, he championed what he called the "cultural convergence" of Aboriginal and European traditions as the future of Australian art. His discussion of cultural convergence echoed his claim made a year earlier that "radical" art invoked "an image of a finer past," as this, he said, was a feature of contemporary Aboriginal Papunya artists "who adopted modern materials in order to perpetuate a traditional symbolism" and urban-based Aboriginal artists such as Trevor Nickolls. From the latter, he believed, "the most powerful moves towards a convergence of the two cultures might spring" because "it is likely to consist in a large measure in their personal rediscovery of a lost Aboriginal past . . . [which] is one of the most potent ways in which mythical elements work in any cultural situation."[105]

However, this was not enough for Smith to include either of these Aboriginal art movements in the radical tradition of Australian art, as if his former exclusion of Aboriginal art continued to frame his idea of Australian art. If, as he wrote in 1998, he had "become less enthusiastic about the notion of 'national' art as I have grown older," he became increasingly protective of his legacy.[106] Insisting that the convergence of Aboriginal and European traditions did not alter his history of Australian art, which had conveniently ended in 1970, in his last years he opposed the tendency of new generation critics to "Aboriginalise" Australian art before 1970.[107] To do so, he said, yields to "the fatal temptation . . . to anachronize history in a futile attempt to redeem it."[108] Smith refused to accept that before 1970 Aboriginal art was of the same time, place, and modernity that yielded his histories of Australian art. In the 1980s he sought to redeem Nietzsche's and Lindsay's Australian legacy, but now, as we pass the sesquicentenary of the publication of *The Birth of Tragedy*, it is neither Nietzsche nor Lindsay, redeemed or not, that are relevant to either Smith's legacy or the future of Australian art. Now it will be judged in the context of what he called in his last published essay, "the modernisation of Australian Indigenous art."[109]

1 Bernard Smith, "Notes on Elitism and the Arts," in *The Death of the Artist as Hero: Essays in History and Culture* (Oxford University Press, 1988), 3–4.

2 Bernard Smith, "City Lights," *The Times Literary Supplement*, no. 3865, 9 April 1976, 423.

3 Bernard Smith, "Jack Lindsay's Marxism," 129.

4 WP 204; Friedrich Nietzsche, *The Will to Power*, trans. Walter Kaufmann and R. J. Hollingdale (Vintage Books, 1968), 120.

5 Norman Lindsay, *My Mask* (Angus and Robertson, 1970), 124.

6 Nietzsche writes in an unpublished note: "One must not feign scientism where it is not yet time to be scientific; but even the real researcher has to rid himself of the vanity of feigning a kind of method that at bottom is not yet timely. Likewise not to 'falsify' things and ideas upon which he has come by other means with a false arrangement of deduction and dialectic. Thus Kant in his 'morality' falsifies his innermost psychological inclination; a more recent example is Herbert Spencer's ethics. — One should not conceal and ruin the fact of how our thoughts have come to us. The profoundest and most inexhaustible books will probably always have something of the aphoristic and abrupt character of Pascal's *Pensees*. The driving forces and valuations have been beneath the surface for a long time; what emerges is effect." *The Complete Works of Friedrich Nietzsche*, ed. Alan Schrift, trans. Adrian Del Caro, vol. 16, *Unpublished Fragments (Spring 1885–86)* (Stanford University Press, 2020), 91.

7 Letter to Lou, August 8–24, 1882, "Nietzsche's letters 1882," *The Nietzsche Channel*. http://www.thenietzschechannel.com/correspondence/eng/nlett-1882.htm

8 Walter Kaufmann, "Introduction," in Friedrich Nietzsche, "On the Geneology of Morals," in *On the Geneology of Morals; Ecce Homo*, ed. Walter Kaufmann (Vintage Books, 1967), 6.

9 GS 58. Friedrich Nietzsche, *The Gay Science*, trans. Josefine Nauckhoff (Cambridge University Press, 2001), 69–70.

10 EH, "Why I am So Wise," 1; Friedrich Nietzsche, *Ecce Homo*, trans. Anthony M. Ludovici (Macmillan, 1911), 12.

11 EH, "Why I am So Wise," 3; Friedrich Nietzsche, "Ecce Homo: How to Become What You Are," in *The Anti-Christ, Ecce Homo, Twilight of the Idols, and Other Writings*, ed. Aaron Ridley and Judith Norman (Cambridge University Press, 2005), 77.

12 EH, "Why I am So Wise," 3.

13 EH, "Why I Write Such Good Books," "Thus Spoke Zarathustra," 3.

14 Z, "Of the Friend"; Friedrich Nietzsche, *Thus Spoke Zarathustra: A Book for All and None*, trans. Alexander Tille (The Macmillan Company, 1896), 73.

15 HH 4.

16 Z, "The Second Dance-Song."

17 WP 131.

18 Jack Lindsay, *Dionysos: Nietzsche Contra Nietzsche: An Essay in Lyrical Philosophy* (Fanfrolico Press, 1928), 4.

19 Jack Lindsay, *The Fullness of Life: Autobiography of an Idea*, ed. Anne Cranny-Francis (c. 1970), 1.1.

20 Lindsay, *The Fullness of Life*, 1.5–6.
21 Jack Lindsay, "Zarathustra in Queensland," *Meanjin* 7, no. 4 (1948): 223.
22 Lindsay, "Zarathustra in Queensland," 222. See also Jack Lindsay, *Life Rarely Tells* (The Bodley Head, 1958), 202.
23 Jack Lindsay, *The Anatomy of Spirit: An Inquiry into the Origins of Religious Emotion* (Methuen, 1937), 3, 6.
24 Lindsay, *The Anatomy of Spirit*, 15.
25 Jack Lindsay, *A Short History of Culture* (Victor Gollancz, 1939), 58.
26 Lindsay, *The Fullness of Life*, 10.33–34.
27 Lindsay, *Life Rarely Tells*, 204–05.
28 N. Lindsay, "The Red Page," *The Bulletin*, 15 September 1904.
29 Bernard Smith, *The Spectre of Truganini, 1980 Boyer Lectures* (Australian Broadcasting Commission, 1980), 22.
30 Bernard Smith, *Modernism's History: A Study of Twentieth-Century Art and Ideas* (UNSW Press, 1998), 55.
31 Friedrich Nietzsche, "On the Uses and Disadvantages of History for Life," in *Untimely Meditations* (Cambridge University Press, 1997), 61.
32 Nietzsche, "On the Uses and Disadvantages of History for Life," 76.
33 [Norman Lindsay, and Jack Lindsay], "Foreword," *Vision: A Literary Quarterly*, no. 1 (May 1923): 2–3.
34 Lindsay, *A Short History of Culture*, 129.
35 Norman Lindsay, *Creative Effort: An Essay in Affirmation* (Art in Australia, 1920), 30.
36 Lindsay, *Creative Effort*, 6.
37 Lou Salomé, *Nietzsche*, trans. Siegfried Mandel (Urbana and University of Illinois Press, 2001), 121.
38 BT, "An Attempt at Self-criticism," 5; BT 24; Friedrich Nietzsche, *The Birth of Tragedy or Hellenism and Pessimism*, trans. Wm. A. Haussmann (George Allen & Unwin, 1923), 5, 183.
39 BT, "Foreword to Richard Wagner."
40 WP 820.
41 Lindsay, *Creative Effort*, 30.
42 Lindsay, 126.
43 Lindsay, 234.
44 Lindsay, *Life Rarely Tells*, 176.
45 Lindsay, 206.
46 Lindsay, "Foreword," 3.
47 Lindsay, *Creative Effort*, 244–46.
48 BT 24.
49 WP 853.
50 GS 4.
51 GS 59.
52 GS 64.
53 GS 4.
54 GM 3.6.
55 WP 815.
56 Lindsay, *Dionysos: Nietzsche Contra Nietzsche: An Essay in Lyrical Philosophy*, 173–74.

57 BGE 239; Friedrich Nietzsche, *Beyond Good and Evil*, trans. Judith Norman (Cambridge University Press, 2002), 129.
58 Rudolph Binion, *Frau Lou: Nietzsche's Wayward Disciple* (Princeton University Press, 1968), 129. Nietzsche, *Beyond Good and Evil*, 69.
59 Jacques Derrida, *Spurs Nietzsche's Styles/Eperons: Les Styles de Nietzsche*, trans. Barbara Harlow (The University of Chicago Press, 1979), 57.
60 For example, Jean Graybeal, *Language and "the Feminine" in Nietzsche and Heidegger* (Indiana University Press, 1990); Paul Patton, ed., *Nietzsche, Feminism and Political Theory* (Routledge, 1993).
61 Z, "On the Friend."
62 BGE, "Preface."
63 BGE 232.
64 WP 812.
65 Keith Ansell-Pearson, "Nietzsche, Woman and Political Theory," in *Nietzsche, Feminism and Political Theory*, ed. Paul Patton (Routledge, 1993), 36.
66 Smith, *Modernism's History: A Study of Twentieth-Century Art and Ideas*, 302.
67 Bernard Smith, "Notes on Abstract Art," in *The Death of the Artist as Hero: Essays in History and Culture* (Oxford University Press, 1988), 187.
68 Smith, "Notes on Abstract Art," 188–89.
69 Bernard Smith, "City Lights," *The Times Literary Supplement*, no. 3865, 9 April 1976, 423.
70 Smith, *The Spectre of Truganini*, 22.
71 Smith, 10.
72 Bernard Smith, "Introduction: A Bibliographic Memoir," in *The Writings of Bernard Smith, Bibliography 1938–1998*, ed. John Spencer, and Peter Wright (Power Publications, 2000), 12.
73 Smith, *The Spectre of Truganini*, 22.
74 Lindsay, *The Fullness of Life*, 15.
75 Lindsay, *Life Rarely Tells*, 207.
76 Lindsay, 208.
77 Smith, "Jack Lindsay," 108.
78 Smith, 108.
79 Peter Beilharz, *Imagining the Antipodes: Culture, Theory, and the Visual in the Work of Bernard Smith* (Cambridge University Press, 1997), 187.
80 Beilharz, *Imagining the Antipodes*, 187.
81 Smith, "The Truth About the Antipodeans," 213.
82 "The Antipodean Manifesto," 197, 95.
83 Sheridan Palmer, *Hegel's Owl: The Life of Bernard Smith* (Power Publications, 2016), 39–45.
84 Bernard Smith, *Place, Taste and Tradition: A Study of Australian Art since 1788*, 2nd ed. (Oxford University Press, 1979), 16.
85 Smith, *Place, Taste and Tradition*, 276.
86 Smith, 280.
87 Smith, 174.
88 Smith, 170.
89 Smith, 174–75.

90 Smith, 20.
91 Bernard Smith, with Terry Smith, *Australian Painting 1788–1990* (Oxford University Press, 1991), 107.
92 Smith, *Place, Taste and Tradition*, 28. See also Ian McLean, *Double Nation: A History of Australian Art* (Reaktion Books, 2023), 19–20.
93 Smith, *Place, Taste and Tradition*, 95–99, 175–77.
94 Smith, "Is There a Radical Tradition in Australian Art?," 231–32.
95 Smith, 233.
96 Smith, 240.
97 Smith, 233–34
98 Smith, 235–39.
99 Smith, 235–36.
100 Palmer, *Hegel's Owl*, 317–23.
101 Julie Copeland, "Bernard Smith a Reluctant Icon," *Artlink* 26, no. 4 (2006): 84.
102 Smith, "Is There a Radical Tradition in Australian Art?," 239.
103 Smith, 236.
104 Smith, *Australian Painting 1788–1990*, 379.
105 Smith, "On Cultural Convergence," 296.
106 Smith, "Introduction: A Bibliographic Memoir," 3.
107 Subsequent updates of *Australian Painting* in 1991 and 2001 by other authors, follow this prescription.
108 Smith, "Introduction: A Bibliographic Memoir," 4. See Ian McLean, "Bernard Smith's Blind Spot: Aboriginal and Australian Art," in *The Legacies of Bernard Smith: Essays on Australian Art, History and Cultural Politics*, ed. Jaynie Anderson, Christopher R. Marshall, and Andrew Yip (Power Publications and Art Gallery of NSW, 2016).
109 Bernard Smith, "Creators and Catalysts: The Modernisation of Australian Indigenous Art," *Australian Cultural History* 26 (2006).

Taking Flight from Oneself: Nietzsche on the Poets, Baudelaire, and the Little Parisian Decadents

Keith Ansell-Pearson

Taking Flight from Oneself

Appreciations of Nietzsche as a "poet-philosopher" reveal little about his thinking concerning the poets. I offer a corrective in this essay by examining how he figures the task of the poets in his middle writings and highlighting the character of his critical treatment of modern French writers and poets. His criticism of the poets is that they are fundamentally melancholic and too readily give vent to naturalising impulses. At the same time, Nietzsche recognises the significance of poets when they assume the task of providing signposts to the future and developing images of what he calls "beautiful human beings." Nietzsche's middle writings (1878–82) form the focus of this first section of the essay. The texts that make up his middle period—five texts in total—should not be regarded as a homogeneous set. Rather, there takes place in the writings subtle but significant shifts in his thinking on the various topics he is handling in them. This is the case with his views on the poets during this period. In the second section of the essay, I show that the writings of Stifter are important for an appreciation of Nietzsche on two fronts: for the notion of beautiful humans and for the concern with decadence. In the third section of the essay, I turn my attention to Nietzsche's focus on art and the poets in his late writings, where it is the notion of decadence that informs and steers his treatments of them, with a special focus on modern French novelists and poets. I shall devote special attention to Baudelaire for reasons that will become clear.

We witness in the middle writings a deep break in Nietzsche's thinking, where *Human, All Too Human* is said by him to be a "monument to a crisis."[1] One major shift that takes place in Nietzsche's thinking from the early writings to the middle writings is his changing attitude towards art. For example, whereas in *The Birth of Tragedy* and the four *Unfashionable Observations* it is art that dominates his thinking about culture—be it the artist's metaphysics of *The Birth of Tragedy* or the need to will illusion in the unfashionable observations—in the middle writings it is "the passion of knowledge" (*die Leidenschaft der Erkenntniss*) that now governs his thinking, and this necessarily means that art is now valued by Nietzsche differently to the valuation we find in his early writings; indeed, Nietzsche posits in *The Birth of Tragedy* an "artist's *metaphysics*."[2] In *Human, All Too Human* Nietzsche lets it be known that he maintains that there has not yet been any philosopher who has not eventually looked down upon the philosophy he invented in his youth with disdain, or at least with suspicion.[3] In an unpublished note from 1877, he wants to make clear to his readers that he has abandoned the metaphysical-artistic views of his early writings.[4] In particular, he wants to overcome what he calls the "deliberate holding on to illusion" as a foundation of culture.[5] Nietzsche is seeking to overcome what he calls Jesuitism, which he located in his predecessors in German philosophy and himself. In the words of one commentator, this means not allowing the uncovering of the limits of human knowledge to be conducted in such a way that the task also gives free rein to metaphysics and the metaphysical need, which is the need to ask the so-called big questions concerning first and last things.[6]

In his *Selbskritik* of 1886, written as a preface to his first book, Nietzsche shows himself to be an astute critic of his own writings. He looks back on his youthful first book, *The Birth of Tragedy*, and finds it "an impossible book . . . image-mazed and image-crazed," hinting at the fact there is a distinct lack of clarity in its usage of concepts. He has moved on from it, even if some of his readers to this day have not. Indeed, he writes perspicaciously of its lack of "logical cleanliness"; it is, he says, "sugary to the point of effeminacy," and "too arrogant to prove its assertions"—in short, it manifests bad philosophy.[7] This doesn't mean it may not be posing some vitally important questions. Nietzsche reveals in his preface what they might be: is pessimism necessarily a sign of weakness, of decline and decay? Might there be a pessimism of strength, and that would consist in having an intellectual predilection for the hard, gruesome, and problematic aspects of existence, but also one that comes from abundance and a feeling of well-being? Might science (*Wissenschaft*) and scientific method be a fear of and flight from pessimism, a subtle defence *against* truth?[8] Put in moral terms, science would then be a form of insincerity; put in immoral terms, it might be a form of cunning.[9] Finally, in contrast and in opposition to romantic art and romantic music (read: Wagner), as well as Christianity, in this preface, Nietzsche calls for an art of comfort *in this world*, and one that will embolden pessimists to live and flourish as *laughing* pessimists.[10] The seduction offered by Wagner's art needs to be resisted, since it flatters every nihilistic-Buddhistic instinct and disguises it in music. Moreover, he "flatters every aspect of Christianity, every form in which religion expresses decadence."[11]

Nietzsche on Art and the Poets in the Middle Writings

In aphorism 148 of *Human, All Too Human*, poets are said to exist to ease life and their gaze is typically directed backwards toward the past. Nietzsche holds we can employ them, albeit unproductively, "as bridges to far away times and ideas, to dying or deceased religions and cultures. They are, in fact, always and necessarily *epigones*." In seeking to make our lives easier, poets either turn our gaze away from the toilsome present or aid the present by shining a light upon it from the past, and it is this preoccupation with the past and bygone times that serves to turn them into deeply melancholic figures. In the second volume of *Human, All Too Human*, featuring "Mixed Opinions and Maxims" and "The Wanderer and His Shadow," Nietzsche alters the view he adopted in the first volume and now enunciates his expectation of today's poets, invoking a poetry of the future and assigning to poets a specific task. The new role he assigns to the poet is not to portray present times or to reanimate and condense the past, but rather to intimate the future. The poet is to do this by composing and recomposing images of beautiful human beings and indicating that such humans are still possible "*in the midst* of our modern world." This is not an easy task when we consider what Nietzsche says in aphorism 111 of *Mixed Opinions and Maxims*, chiefly that today's poets live in too close a proximity to "the sewers of the big cities." This theme is continued in aphorism 283 of *The Gay Science* where he writes of the need for preparatory courageous human beings—which echoes the preparatory task he assigns to the new poets—and who cannot emerge out of "the sand and slime of present-day civilisation and metropolitanism," but rather who must exist at the present time patiently and cheerfully like shy deer in the forests.[12]

For Nietzsche, too many poets reveal an impatience with themselves, and are gloomy on account of their desire to take flight from themselves (he mentions the likes of Byron and Musset); they "resemble stampeding horses, who glean from their own creative work only a short-lived joy and ardor that virtually explodes their veins before falling into so wintery a desolation and woebegoneness."[13] The poets thirst to dissolve outside themselves, or to dissolve into God and become completely one with him, or, as in the case of Shakespeare, Nietzsche adds, "into images of the most passionate life."[14] The poet might even thirst for deeds as a way of diverting the self from itself, as Nietzsche finds in the case of Byron. This suggests to him that in the most extreme examples we encounter of someone disclosing in their behaviour this drive for action at any price and no matter how reckless, we need to consult the knowledge and experience of the psychiatrist. Nietzsche laments the fact that, as he sees it, poets are no longer teachers. Aphorism 172 in *Mixed Opinions and Maxims* is devoted to exploring this topic: "However strange it may seem to our age: there were once poets and artists whose souls were beyond the passions, with their convulsions and raptures, and who therefore took pleasure in purer materials, worthier human beings, more delicate combinations and solutions."[15] Today, Nietzsche reflects, all the talk amongst artists is on unchaining the will, liberating life, and smashing things. In previous ages, however, the artist was conceived as a tamer of the will, a transformer of animals, and a creator and sculptor of human beings. Whereas the ancient Greeks saw the poet as a teacher of adults, as someone who himself "became a good poem or a beautiful creation," today we are presented with art that is the reflection, even celebration, of little more than "a cave of desires, ruinously overgrown with flowers, prickly plants and poisonous weeds," so presenting the thinker with an object for melancholy reflection and because the "most noble and most precious now grow up already in ruins."[16]

Informing Nietzsche's consideration of the poet is a quite specific conception of the role and task of art, and one that he is keen to hold onto. He contests the idea that the artwork of the artist is the real thing and is all that matters. Against this modern idea, he wants us to see and appreciate the artwork as an appendage of life. Art should exist, he ventures, first and foremost to embellish life, aiding the task of making ourselves tolerable to ourselves and pleasing to others: "with this task before its eyes, it restrains and reins us in, creates forms for social intercourse, binds ill-bred people to the laws of propriety, purity, politeness, of speaking and keeping silent at the right time."[17] Furthermore, art needs to focus its energy on concealing and reinterpreting everything ugly, "those painful, frightening, disgusting things that will, despite all our efforts, break out again and again in accordance with the descent of human nature."[18] In particular, and with regard to this focus, art needs to address the problems presented by human passions, "to the soul's pains and fears and allow the *meaning* behind whatever is unavoidably or insurmountably ugly to shine through."[19] A human being, therefore, who feels within him or herself a surplus of "embellishing, concealing, and reinterpreting energies" will "seek to discharge this surplus in artworks."[20] In aphorism 177, Nietzsche discloses his interest in the perfecting of the human animal and with reference to the task of art, and he ends this aphorism by noting that it is perhaps the Greeks who, in the ideal of Athena, cast their gaze the farthest of any human being thus far.[21] The nature of the appeal he makes here to the female warrior Athena is perhaps obvious: she represents for him a figure of unity, namely, the unity of culture involving justice, wisdom, and the arts. In aphorism 173 of the same text, he conceives of art as the energetic surplus of a wise and harmonious individual:

> *Forward and backward glance.* An art as it flows forth from Homer, Sophocles, Theocritus, Calderón, Racine, Goethe as the *surplus* of a wise and harmonious mode of life—that is the right sort of art, toward which we finally learn to reach when we have ourselves become wiser and more harmonious,

> not the barbaric, however delightful bubbling over of heated and brightly colored things from an untamed, chaotic soul, which we had earlier, as youths, understood to be art.[22]

With these insights into Nietzsche's thinking about art in mind, let me now turn to his conception of a poetry of the future. Aphorism 99 of *Mixed Opinions and Maxims* is entitled "The Poet as a Signpost to the Future." He proposes that all the surplus poetic strength that is available to contemporary human beings needs to be dedicated to a principal single goal, namely, not simply portraying present times, and most definitely not seeking to reanimate and condense the past, but rather showing the way to a possible future. The poet's task is clearly not that of an imaginative political scientist who seeks to anticipate in their images more favourable social and cultural conditions that might then give rise to new human beings; rather, the poet needs to take their lead from artists of earlier times who sought to compose and recompose images of divine human beings. Now, though, the task is to create images of beautiful human beings, sniffing out cases where "*in the midst of*" the modern world, and without withdrawing from reality, the beautiful and great spirit can be found. If poets commit themselves to this task, they will help to create the future. In writing their poems, the new poets will be distinguished, he goes on to elaborate, "by seeing to be closed off from and protected against the breath and heat of the *passions*."

Nietzsche then spells out the reasons as to why he holds to this view. If the poets focus on "smashing the entire human frame," they will be overburdened by such a task and may well end up producing little more than mocking laughter and "gnashing their teeth," simply because they will be dealing with "everything tragic and comic in the usual old sense." In short, the danger of the poets who pursue the task set in this way will be one of indulging in cynicism and promoting despair, and so allowing a mood of profound melancholy to take root. Instead, Nietzsche encourages poets to develop the "innate sense of moderation," along with strength and mildness, cultivating "a level ground that gives rest and pleasure to the foot, a shining heaven mirrored in faces and events," and in which knowledge and art flow together into a new unity. What is needed from the poets is "the grace of seriousness," not "the impatience of division" (the former aims at integrity or wholeness, the latter is content with being an actor). He ends the aphorism by referring to this art of the poets as being informed by an "inclusive, general, golden background" upon which, and for the first time, "the delicate *differences* among embodied ideals would make up the actual *painting*—that of an ever-increasing majesty." Although several paths lead to this poetry of the future from the example of Goethe, there remains the need for many more "good pathfinders," and a greater power than can be found in today's poets, who are little more than "inoffensive depicters of semi-animals and of an immaturity and immoderation that they confuse with force and nature." The poets will help to build the future by composing images of beautiful and great spirits that will stimulate envy and imitation. Such spirits will be shown embodying themselves "in harmonious, well-proportioned circumstances," revealing "visibility, durability, and exemplarity."

His suspicion about the poets continues to express itself in the writings of his late period, such as *Beyond Good and Evil* (see aphorism 269, where he refers to the likes of Byron, Musset, Poe, Leopardi, Kleist, and Gogol). His impatience is well expressed in this note from 1885: "Against false idealism, where exaggerated subtlety alienates the best natures in the world. What a pity that the whole of southern Europe has lost the inheritance of that bound sensuality through the abstinence of the clergy! And it's fair that such Shelleys, Hölderlins, Leopardis perish, I don't think much of such people. It amuses me to think of the revenge that the rough naturalness of nature takes in such people, e.g., when I hear that Leopardi used to masturbate and later became impotent."[23]

The Relevance of Stifter

Although some critics have argued that Nietzsche's remarks on decadence are riddled with contradiction, to the point, it is claimed, where they fail to coalesce into useful insight, his analysis of decadence is the pivot around which turns Nietzsche's critical insights into modernity and that inform and guide his conception of philosophical activity in the late writings.[24] I hold that an undetected influence on Nietzsche's taking seriously the problem of decadence are the writings of the Austrian novelist and poet Adalbert Stifter, of whom he was a great admirer. According to Ernst Bertram, the main inspiration on Nietzsche with regard to the idea of beautiful human beings comes from the writings of Stifter, especially his novel, *Indian Summer* (*Der Nachsommer*), first published in 1857.[25] Indeed, we find extensive discussions of beauty in Stifter's novel, along with appeals to the creation of beautiful human figures in painting and in art in general. As Martin and Erika Swales note in their study, reflecting on Nietzsche's interest in Stifter, it at first sight seems an unlikely meeting of minds. They venture the explanation that Nietzsche was well attuned to the *unzeitgemäss* impulses informing Stifter's art, and that he admired him "because of what he perceived as the embattled integrity of his art, its uncompromising transcendence of the tangle and turmoil of human passion, its willed calm and repose beyond heartbreak and weariness."[26] In addition, they note what Bertram also sees in Nietzsche's appreciation of Stifter's letters: "Nietzsche esteemed Stifter's fierce resistance to his times, to their banality and meretriciousness."[27]

Although Stifter's influence on Nietzsche is at its strongest in his middle writings, notably key aphorisms in *Mixed Opinions and Maxims*, his admiration of him is revealed in his notebooks of the late period. For example, in reflecting on what is born in the nineteenth century from relative plenitude, he remarks, revealing a self-confidence, "among poets, e.g., Stifter and Gottfried Keller are signs of greater strength, inner well-being."[28] Moreover, in a note from October–November 1888, Nietzsche discloses that *Indian Summer* is the only German book after Goethe that has magic for him.[29] The Indian summer in Stifter's novel, completed when he was fifty-two years old, refers to the blossoming time of one's life, the time when the roses cultivated through many hard years of toil burst forth in full bloom.[30] It is precisely this time Nietzsche is referring to in the note of October-November 1888 when he writes of an autumnal mood of the soul, golden and sweetening, telling of an October sun of profound serenity. In aphorism 338 of *The Wanderer and His Shadow*, Nietzsche writes of the constantly sunny October air as an atmosphere where Italy and Finland "have come together in union, in a place that seems to be home to all the silvery tints of nature:—how happy is he who can say: 'There is certainly much that is greater and more beautiful in nature, but *this* I find to be intimate and familiar to me, related by blood, indeed, even more than that.'"[31] We can also note the way Nietzsche depicts this mood and experience in "Of the Blissful Isles" in part two of *Thus Spoke Zarathustra*: "Thus, like figs do these teachings fall to you, my friends: now drink their juice and eat their sweet flesh! It is autumn all around and clear sky and afternoon. Behold what abundance is around us! And it is fine to gaze out upon distant seas from the midst of superfluity."

In the published writings, it is in *The Wanderer and His Shadow* that Nietzsche expresses his admiration for Stifter's book. If we leave to one side the writings of Goethe, especially the conversations with Eckermann, "the best German book that exists," Nietzsche writes, then, he continues, there remains only four German books that merit being read again and again: "Lichtenberg's aphorisms, the first book of Jung-Stilling's biography, Adalbert Stifter's *Nachsommer* and Gottfried Keller's *Leute von Seldwyla*."[32] In Bertram's incisive appreciation, Nietzsche is seen, in fact, as being more strongly affected by the pedagogical utopia depicted in Stifter's *Indian Summer* than he was by an Eckermann mood of late classicism and humanism, and whose end Nietzsche intuited and saw reflected in Stifter's novel in terms of a melancholy transfiguration.[33] In the novel, Nietzsche would have found references to several poets of concern to him, including Homer, Shakespeare,[34] and Goethe, along with discussions between the main characters on a range of topics that, we can surmise, resonated deeply with him, including reflections on the need to approach the study of the human animal and its history through the lens of the natural sciences, on the importance of beauty in life, on the role of the poets, on the nature of philosophy, and on the need to become a master of one's emotions. In the chapter entitled "Die Erweiterung" in the novel *Indian Summer*, the poets are referred to as the greatest benefactors of mankind, indeed, as "the priests of the beautiful" (*die Priester des Schönen*).[35] According to one commentator, love of beauty, including nature, the human body, art, and human relations, is the basic theme of the novel.[36]

Stifter saw himself not as a Goethe but simply as one of Goethe's kin, and in his writings "the seed of the pure, noble, simple goes out to men's hearts" to direct their minds and lives away from the "odious, disgusting nihilism" that surrounds them.[37] Indeed, in the preface to *Motley Stones*, Stifter anticipates the principal features of decadence that will come to occupy so much of the thinking to be found in Nietzsche's late texts, such as *Twilight of the Idols*, *The Case of Wagner*, and *The Antichrist*:

> Declining peoples first lose their sense of moderation. They strive for isolated particulars, they fling themselves shortsightedly on narrow and trifling things, they raise the conditional above the universal . . . their art depicts what is one-sided what is valid from one perspective only, then what is disjointed dissonant bizarre, eventually what excites and tantalizes the senses . . . the individual scorns the whole, pursuing his pleasure and his ruin.[38]

Nietzsche on Baudelaire and the Little Parisian Decadents

From the late period, let me focus initially on Nietzsche's approach to the case of Wagner. In the preface to *The Case of Wagner*, he appeals to philosophy in a quite specific sense. He does not wish to write as a moralist with respect to Wagner's case, but to reach a level of understanding that is beyond moralistic judgement and appraisal. Wagner is a decadent, in fact, a "typical" one,[39] and Nietzsche wishes to understand the nature of this decadence. He knows Wagner's art intimately, so he is well qualified to write on it, but he also knows himself to be a child of his time and hence something of a decadent too. The task, though, is to become timeless and overcome one's age: to see through it and hopefully indicate possibilities or openings beyond it.[40]

Decadence can be understood in several senses, and when Nietzsche first introduces the notion in *The Case of Wagner* it is in the sense of morality as "declining life" and "impoverished life": "the will to the end, the great exhaustion."[41] What is held to be sick are Schopenhauer's philosophy, Wagner's art, and modern humaneness, and decadence is discovered to be the art *par excellence* of modern metropolitan existence. Nietzsche understands his own Wagnerism as one of his sicknesses. He aims, however, to be philosophical about modern decadence by securing an appropriately superior viewpoint on it, practising "a profoundly cold and sober attitude" and "an eye that looks out over the whole fact of humanity from a tremendous distance."[42] Nietzsche is pursuing, in fact, a complex art of diagnostic philosophy: the concern is with health, but this health is implicated in sickness, and Wagner's case is seen as paradigmatic of the age, of modernity. This explains why Nietzsche says that the philosopher cannot do without Wagner, including the harmful effects of his art: the philosopher "has to be the bad conscience of his age,— and that is why he needs to know it best." To delve into the malaise that is Wagnerism, then, is to examine the labyrinth of the modern soul: "Modernity speaks its most *intimate* language in Wagner."[43] To know modernity for Nietzsche, is to work through Wagner, and therefore at the end of the book he can say, and not only with a dose of sarcasm, that it is a text written out of gratitude.

The way Nietzsche seeks to develop an understanding of the phenomenon of Wagner is in terms of what he takes to be the very *pathos* of philosophy, which is to be conceived as a certain kind of view from above in which the whole is surveyed, as in "the great problems close enough to grasp; the world surveyed as if from a mountain."[44] Nevertheless, his critique of Wagner and his music is stated powerfully and from the perspective of Nietzsche's deep-seated worries about modern existence. Wagner, he holds, "shrouds the blackest obscurantism inside the light of the ideal," and in the process he "flatters every nihilistic (-Buddhistic) instinct and disguises it in music." Moreover, he "flatters every aspect of Christianity, every form in which religion expresses decadence."[45] In *Nietzsche contra Wagner*, Nietzsche locates in *Parsifal* a "return to sickly Christian and obscurantist ideals . . ."[46] Ultimately, then, what grows on the soil of impoverished life is "the whole counterfeit of transcendence and beyond," and that finds its most sublime advocate in Wagner's art."[47] His art does this not through formulas, but through a "persuading sensuality" that makes the spirit brittle and tired. For Nietzsche, it is another form of modern weakness, like modernity's weak scepticism.[48]

In *Nietzsche contra Wagner*, Nietzsche connects the problems that characterise Wagner's art and its mythical content to the problems that interest those he calls "the little Parisian decadents," and states with biting wit: "Always five steps away from the hospital! Entirely modern, entirely *metropolitan* problems! Don't doubt it."[49] Nietzsche was extremely well-read in the literature and thought of nineteenth-century France, and with respect to decadents, his focus is on Baudelaire, who he holds to be the first "intelligent" follower of Wagner and another typical decadent.[50] Nietzsche typically interprets the "little Parisians," literary figures such as Baudelaire and Flaubert, as writers who display "pessimistic attitudes." He regards Baudelaire as "just as German as Parisian; his poetry has something of what in Germany is called *Gemüt* or 'endless melody' and sometimes also 'caterwauling' . . . There is much Wagner in Baudelaire."[51] Baudelaire is a human being who was "ruined," but who also, as a critic and poet, had "sharp taste" that was sure of itself, and with this "he tyrannizes the insecure of today."[52] Ultimately, Nietzsche will question, and question Schopenhauer especially on this point, whether there is such a thing as genuinely pessimistic art: "Tragedy does *not* teach 'resignation'—To represent terrible and questionable things is in itself an instinct for power and magnificence in an artist: he does not fear them . . . Art affirms . . .

—But Zola?"[53] His critical point is that even when an artist like Zola displays ugliness, he is taking "*pleasure in the ugly*," and to think otherwise is to deceive oneself. Writing "against the romanticism of great 'passion,'" Nietzsche argues that the task is not for art to play with artistic formulas, but to "remodel life so that afterward it *has* to formulate itself."[54] Art can be the consequence of a soul dissatisfied with reality, as he finds in the romantic pessimism of a great deal of modern art, but it can also be "an expression of *gratitude for happiness enjoyed*."[55] He identifies the former with romanticism and the latter with aureole (*Glorien-schein*) and dithyramb, and mentions in connection with the latter "art of apotheosis" the diverse likes of Rubens, Hafiz, and Goethe. He contrasts this "blissful" and "graceful" art of "eternalization" with its opposite that is governed by the tyrannical will of the great sufferer from life, who forges "what is most personal, individual, and narrow . . . in his suffering, into a binding *law* and compulsion, taking revenge on all things, as it were, by impressing, forcing, and branding into them his image, the image of his torture."[56]

Nowhere in his published writings, though, does Nietzsche take note of Baudelaire's defence of the literature of his generation from the charge of producing a literature of decadence. Baudelaire finds the phrase little more than "empty words" that "fall with a pompous yawn from the lips of the sphinxes without a riddle that guard the holy portals of classical aesthetics."[57] Moreover, he argues that it is a dubious term to deploy as a piece of criticism because it supposes there is some objective scale of literatures that can be considered from the vantage point of a presumed providential process, one that accuses certain writers and poets of rejoicing in their own miserable destiny. Contra such a pompous stance, Baudelaire sounds almost like Nietzsche when he writes of a new dawn in which "some poetic minds will find new joys . . . a paradise of fire, a melancholy splendour . . . all the magic of dreams, all the memories of opium . . . the sunset will then appear to them as the marvellous allegory of a soul, imbued with life, going down beyond the horizon, with a magnificent wealth of thoughts and dreams."[58]

Walter Benjamin maintains, in contrast to Nietzsche's perception, that Baudelaire is *not* a pessimist, and that spleen serves as a bulwark against pessimism: "This is because, with Baudelaire, a taboo is placed on the future."[59] He rightly notes that this is what distinguishes his heroism from Nietzsche's. Benjamin proposes that we conceive Baudelaire not as a pessimist but as an incomparable "brooder," and this figure, he suggests, is a historically distinct type of thinker that "is at home among allegories."[60] Furthermore, Benjamin conceives the heroic bearing of Baudelaire as, in fact, intimately related to Nietzsche: "Although Baudelaire adheres to Catholicism, his experience of the universe is in exact accord with the experience comprehended by Nietzsche in the phrase 'God is dead.'"[61] What we see here is Benjamin's ultimate explanation of Baudelaire's melancholy.[62] The difference with Nietzsche, however, is readily discernible, since we know that for him the monstrous event of the death of God that is on its way is not to be a source for our melancholy but interpreted as a sign of *Heiterkeit*, that is, of cheerfulness and serenity that come to us as rewards,[63] as hard-won victories, and that provide us with feelings of expectation and anticipation—in short, the charting of "new seas."[64]

Of equal interest to a consideration of the problems of modernity is the figuration of dandyism we find in Baudelaire's 1863 essay on "The Painter of Modern Life." As Leo Bersani notes in a consideration of the interpretation of Baudelaire by Jeffrey Mehlman, the prince-dandy can be construed as a kind of Nietzschean hero.[65] It is a possible heroic figure not mentioned by Nietzsche in his consideration of Baudelaire. Let me bring out this appreciation of the figure of the dandy even more than Bersani does. As Benjamin notes, Baudelaire considered the dandy to be a descendant of great ancestors, and in his essay on the painter and modern life he refers to Caesar, Catilina, and Alcibiades as brilliant examples.[66] Benjamin also cites Baudelaire's view that dandyism is "the last flicker of heroism in decadent ages."[67] Baudelaire presents the dandy as a complex hybrid figure—for example, as a mixture of the grave and the gay—and as coming close to a strange form "of spirituality and stoicism too."[68]

We perhaps begin to see the relevance of this figure to Nietzsche's concerns when we take stock of Baudelaire's claim that dandyism appears in periods of transition when democracy is yet to become all-powerful and aristocracy is only partially weakened and discredited. In such a context, outsiders appear who "endowed with native energy" and conceive "the idea of establishing a new kind of aristocracy."[69]

Baudelaire goes on to give his reasons for his melancholy when he writes: "But alas! the rising tide of democracy, which spreads everywhere and reduces everything to the same level, is carrying away these last champions of human pride, and submerging, in the waters of oblivion, the last traces of these remarkable myrmidons."[70] The relevance to Nietzsche is discernible when Baudelaire refers to Chateaubriand finding examples of dandyism "in the forests and lake-sides of the New World,"[71] since it is in the forests that Nietzsche envisages the free-spirited philosopher dwelling as "the enemy of fetters" and "the non-worshipper."[72] We should also recall his appeal to preparatory courageous human beings who have contempt for all the great human vanities and who currently live like shy deer in the forests, "silent, lonely, resolute."[73] Such preparatory human beings cannot emerge from "the sand and slime of present-day civilization and metropolitanism," and so they must live patiently, and even "cheerfully," for the right time to prosper as "more fruitful human beings, happier beings!"[74] Although the reference to the forests here is intended in large part metaphorically, it seems to me that there is an affinity with Baudelaire's hope for a new dandyism within modernity.

Nietzsche construes himself as both a decadent and a new beginning, and to know this of himself, he thinks, is the result of his ability to pursue a superior vista on modernity, what he calls the surveying from above that characterises a certain philosophical *pathos*. Pessimism and the attachment to melancholy cannot be allowed to be given the final say on life; rather, they require a treatment of modernity that is made from higher perspectives, such as the perspective of the philosopher as an interpreter of signs and symptoms; for example, inquiring into whether the "values" of modernity are signs of ascending or declining life. Pessimism can only be granted the last word if we suppose what there is no entitlement to suppose: that all is vanity and that all is over. Regarding those who dwell only or largely on the filthy aspects of human existence, Nietzsche is undaunted, and counters by appealing to the positive effects of the emotion of disgust: "That is why the fanatics and hypocrites with bowed heads whose hearts too are bowed down preach: 'The world itself is a filthy monster' . . . There is much filth in the world: *so much* is true! But the world itself is not yet a filthy monster on that account! There is wisdom in the fact that much in the world smells ill: disgust itself creates wings and water-divining powers!"[75]

The preoccupation Nietzsche has in his late writings with symptomatology and a semiology of morals is informing his remarks on the Parisian decadents—and other kinds of perceived pessimists and nihilists—at a deep level. He invites us to reflect on this question: "Nowadays I avail myself of this primary distinction concerning artists of every kind: is it *hatred* of life or *superabundance* of life that has become creative here?" And in a novelist and writer such as Flaubert—"a new edition of Pascal," he contends—he locates the hatred of life as an instinctive judgement: "He tortured himself when he wrote, just as Pascal tortured himself when he thought—they both felt unegoistic . . . 'Selflessness'—that principle of decadence, the will to the end in art as in morality."[76] To want to flee from oneself in this way, and through the medium of art, is to want to flee from life itself.[77] In fact, Nietzsche has several objections to Flaubert and to French writers. He contends that what motivates them is self-loathing, and a fatalism that provides a certain peace in the face of this self-loathing. We see, then, in their existence as writers, "a flight from the self and forming ideals, making things *better,* through seeking to know how things have *gotten* this way."[78] In seeking to lose themselves in art, writers like Flaubert achieve only "a scientific approach or photography," what Nietzsche describes as "description without perspective," and he adds, with "nothing but foreground and everything cluttered."[79] Moreover, the French novelists describe only "exceptions," and although these are taken from all circles of society, it is the bourgeois that is hated equally by each one of them. Flaubert, Nietzsche observes, was sick and tired of himself as "bourgeois,"[80] and his much lauded "objectivity" is nothing more than a modern means of freeing oneself from scorn.[81] Against this objectivity and "photography" Nietzsche prefers what he calls "great form." This is a form "that looks beyond any single stimulus" and that "is the expression of *great* character," creating the world in its own image, and that is the work of a person of power.[82] On the issue of the "exception," we should bear in mind Nietzsche's thinking about this in an aphorism in *Dawn*: "The rule is more interesting to me than the exception—anyone who feels this way is far advanced in scholarship and belongs to the initiated."[83]

Nietzsche's worry over the desire to flee from the self—which he identifies in several of the French novelists, though not only French writers—seen as evidence of signs of pessimism and decadence, is worth taking seriously and reflecting upon.[84] Christopher Isherwood notes that the atmosphere of Paris was the native element of Baudelaire's inspiration, and cites Baudelaire on his attraction to "the religious intoxication of the great cities."[85] Nietzsche felt that "In the last analysis," the French novelists "can never rid themselves of Paris."[86] He himself preferred the perspective and the clean air of the mountains: "the world surveyed as if from a mountain."[87] And: "Philosophy, as I have understood and lived it so far, is choosing to live in ice and high mountains—seeking out everything alien and questionable in existence . . . Anyone who knows how to breathe in the air of my writings knows that it is an air of the heights, a *bracing* air. You must be made for it, or else you are in no little danger of catching cold in it."[88]

In the case of Baudelaire, might it not be possible though to interpret the new poetry—poetry that sees itself as in an antagonistic relationship with modernity and an enemy of bourgeois mediocrity[89]—as indicating signs of new life? Roger Pearson has recently sought to show that central to Baudelaire's alternative moral vision to the (Roman Catholic) doctrine of sin, and that was deeply embedded in the culture of his day, is the value he accords to human creativity, which Pearson describes as "our active capacity to conjure from the "destruction" wrought by time and depression "new ways of seeing and feeling, new patterns of understanding, new harmonies—in short, what he calls "le Beau" or "la Beauté." Here beauty denotes an "effect of perception . . . a quickening of interest, a sense of new possibilities . . . as they come tantalizingly and intriguingly into view."[90] However, doubts persist when, for example, we read Baudelaire on why, when an exquisite poem brings tears into our eyes, these tears are not to be understood as tears of "an overabundant joy," but rather of "an impatient melancholy, a clamant demand on our nerves, our nature, *exiled in imperfection*, which would fain enter into immediate possession, while still on this earth, of a revealed paradise."[91]

The "exile in imperfection" seems to speak of an irredeemable fallen condition. Despite the theme of melancholy being a prominent one also in Nietzsche, with his commitment to a philosophy of the future, he cannot tolerate the idea that humanity must arrest itself and stagnate at such a hopeless endpoint. In *Ecce Homo* he informs his readers that he is one thing and his writings another thing, which says a great deal about Nietzsche the human being, and almost everything in favour of the human-superhuman visions and riddles to be found in his writings. In the discourse entitled "The Song of Melancholy" in part four of *Thus Spoke Zarathustra*, Nietzsche stages an agon with Zarathustra's adversary the old sorcerer, presented as a "melancholy devil," and at the end of it the lament begins again with Zarathustra admitting, but proudly, that he is "only a fool! only a poet!"

1 This essay utilises material from my forthcoming book *Nietzsche's Earthbound Wisdom: the Poet, and the Sage.* EH, "Human, All Too Human."

2 BT, 5 (my emphasis).

3 HH 253.

4 KSA 8, 23 [159].

5 KSA 10, 16 [23]. Mazzino Montinari, *Reading Nietzsche* (University of Illinois Press, 2003), 60.

6 BT, Preface, 3.

7 BT, Preface, 1.

8 See also Nietzsche's dramatic treatment of the will to truth in *GM* III. He invites us to reflect on the ages in which the scholar predominates: "they are times of exhaustion, often of twilight, of decline,—gone are the overflowing energy, the certainty of life, the certainty as to the *future*" (GM III. 25).

As strange as it may sound, modern science, Nietzsche claims, is, at least for the present time, the best ally of the ascetic ideal, "for the simple reason that it is the most unconscious, involuntary, secret and subterranean" (GM III. 25). Modern science has led man to accept a form of self-contempt: "since Copernicus, man seems to be on a downward path" (GM III. 25). At the end of his classic study *Life against Death* (1959), Norman O'Brown cites from various twentieth-century philosophers, including Alfred North Whitehead and Gaston Bachelard, who identified in science's mercilessly ascetic will to truth the "dominion of death-in-life." He writes: "It is an awe-inspiring attack on the life of the universe; in more technical psychoanalytical terms, its anal-sadistic intent is plain . . . Thus modern science confirms Ferenczi's aphorism: '*Pure intelligence* is thus a product of dying, at least of becoming mentally insensitive, and is therefore *in principle madness*.'" Norman O'Brown, *Life against Death: The Psychoanalytical Meaning of History* (Sphere Books, 1968), 276–7. See also Lewis Mumford, *In the Name of Sanity* (Harcourt, Brace, and Company, 1954), 234: "Science, by definition, has no organ of prophetic anxiety and prophetic foresight, no place in its methodology for dream and form and ideal." The dream of existence is important for the late Nietzsche: "A philosopher: that is a human being who constantly experiences, sees, hears, suspects, hopes, and dreams of extraordinary things . . . A philosopher: oh, a being that often runs away from himself, often is afraid of himself—but is too curious not to "come to himself" again and again" (Nietzsche, BGE 292).

9 BT, Preface, 7.

10 CW, Postscript.

11 GS 283.

12 D 549.

13 D 549.

14 MOM 172.

15 D 549.

16 MOM 174.

17 MOM 174.

18 MOM 174.
19 MOM 174.
20 MOM 177.
21 In MOM 173, Nietzsche stresses an additional insight: "It is self-evident that at certain times of life, an art that is overwrought, agitated, averse to anything orderly, monotonous, simple, or logical is an essential need that artists *must* acknowledge if the soul is not to discharge itself at such times in another way, by all sorts of mischief and bad behaviour."
22 KSA, 11, 34 [95], 451. For instructive insight into Shelley's idealism, see George Santayana, "Shelley: or the Poetic Value of Revolutionary Principles," in *Selected Critical Writings of George Santayana*, vol 1, ed. Norman Henfrey (London & Cambridge University Press, 1968), 157–81. For other references to Shelley in Nietzsche, see SE, 3 and BGE 245.
23 For a critique of Nietzsche on decadence, see Charles Bernheimer, *Decadent Subjects: The Idea of Decadence in Art, Literature, Philosophy, and Culture of the Fin de Siècle in Europe*, ed. T. Jefferson Kline and Naomi Schor (Johns Hopkins University Press, 2002). On Nietzsche and decadence, see also Daniel W. Conway, *Nietzsche's Dangerous Game: Philosophy in the Twilight of the Idols* (Cambridge University Press, 2002); Andrea Gogröf-Voorhees, *Defining Modernism: Baudelaire and Nietzsche on Romanticism, Modernity, Decadence, and Wagner* (Peter Lang, 1999); and Andrew Huddleston, *Nietzsche on the Decadence and Flourishing of Culture* (Oxford University Press, 2019). For a rich study of decadence in nineteenth-century French culture, see Koenraad W. Swart, *The Sense of Decadence in Nineteenth-Century France* (Springer Netherlands, 1964). Nietzsche's conception of decadence is influenced by Paul Bourget's original treatment in his Paul Bourget *Essais de psychologie contemporaine* (Gallimard, 1993) of 1883. Nietzsche refers to Bourget in EH, "Why I Am so Clever," 3. See also Roberto Calasso, *La Folie Baudelaire*, trans. Alistair McEwen (Penguin, 2012), 273–6.
24 Ernst Bertram, *Nietzsche: Attempt at a Mythology*, trans. Robert E. Norton (University of Illinois Press, 2009), first published 1918, 208. In addition to his study of Nietzsche, Bertram was also the author of an earlier appreciation of Stifter. See Ernst Bertram, *Studien zu Adalbert Stifters Novellentechnik* (Dortmund: Fr. Wilh. Ruhfus, 1907).
25 Martin and Erika Swales, *Adalbert Stifter: A Critical Study* (Cambridge University Press, 1984), 22.
26 Swales, *Adalbert Stifter*, 22.
27 KSA 12, 10 [2], 454; WP 1021.
28 KSA 13, 24 [10], 634.
29 Eric A. Blackhall, *Adalbert Stifter: A Critical Study* (Cambridge University Press, 1948), 15.
30 WS 338.
31 WS 109.
32 Ernst, *Studien zu Adalbert*, 208.
33 In the novel, it is *King Lear* that is given prominence. Although there are references to several of Shakespeare's plays in Nietzsche's

corpus, *King Lear* is not one of them. What appeals to the hero of Stifter's novel about the play are the strength of the emotions portrayed and acted out in it, and the fear of going mad.

34 Adalbert Stifter, *Nachsommer*. (Reclam, 2005), 334; Adalbert Stifter, *Indian Summer*, trans. Wendell Frye (Bern: Peter Lang, 2009), 196; see also Adalbert Stifter, *Bunte Steine* (Reclam, 1994), 7; also Adalbert Stifter, *Motley Stones*, trans. Isabel Fargo Cole (New York Review Books), 2021, 3. Here, one might compare Emerson's reflections on the nature and function of the poet "or the man of Beauty": "The sign and credentials of the poet are that he announces that which no man has foretold." Ralph Waldo Emerson, *The Essential Writings of Ralph Waldo Emerson*, ed. Brooks Atkinson (Modern Library, 2000), 290.

35 Margaret Gump, *Adalbert Stifter* (Twayne Publishers, 1974), 99–100.

36 Stifter cited in W. H. Bruford, *The German Tradition of Self-Cultivation: "Bildung" from Humboldt to Thomas Mann* (Cambridge University Press, 1975), 130.

37 Stifter, *Bunte Steine*, 13; Stifter, *Motley Stones*, 8. In the Preface to CW, Nietzsche discloses that the problem that has occupied him the most is the problem of decadence. In Section 5 he refers to the "total sickness," centred on an "over-excitement of the neurological mechanism," and in Section 7 he conceives literary decadence as a situation where "The whole does not live at all anymore: it is cobbled together, calculated, synthetic, and artifact." See also Bourget's classic definition of 1883 in his *Essais de psychologie contemporaine* (Gallimard, 1993), 14, which influenced Nietzsche: "A decadent style is one in which the unity of the book falls apart, replaced by the independence of the sentence, *phrase*, and the sentence makes way for the word." Bourget applies this notion of decadence not only to language, but extends to the organism and to society.

38 CW 5.

39 CW, Preface.

40 CW, Preface.

41 CW, Preface.

42 CW, Preface.

43 CW 1.

44 CW, Postscript.

45 NCW, "Wagner as Apostle of Chastity," 3.

46 CW, Postscript.

47 See BGE 208.

48 CW 9.

49 EH, "Why I Am So Clever," 5; see also TI IX: 3 and KSA 11, 34 [166]; SUP 16, 48. In a letter to his amanuensis Peter Gast, dated February 26, 1888, Nietzsche discloses excitedly that he has been thumbing through a recently published volume of Baudelaire's *Oueuvres posthume*, and has found in it, along with some "invaluable psychological observations relating to *décadence*" an unpublished letter of Wagner's that has caught his eye. The letter is intended for Baudelaire and contains an effusive response to an essay he published in the *Revue Européene* and that Wagner has read:

"a thousand thanks for your beneficence," Wagner writes. This find confirms for Nietzsche what he had suspected for some time but until this discovery had no proof of. Nietzsche cites himself to Gast as follows: "'Who was most ready for Wagner? who was most naturally and inwardly Wagnerian, in spite of and without Wagner?'" In Baudelaire's poems, he reveals to Gast, he had found "a sort of Wagnerian *sensibility*," and goes on to describe him as "a *libertine*, mystical, "satanic," but, above all, Wagnerian." See Christopher Middleton, (1996), *Selected Letters of Friedrich Nietzsche* (Hackett), 286–7. On Baudelaire and the satanic, see T. S. Eliot, "Baudelaire," in *Selected Prose of T. S. Eliot*, ed. Frank Kermode (Faber & Faber, 1975). 234–5.

50 KSA 11, 38 [5], 601; SUP 16, 160. For Baudelaire on Wagner, see Charles Baudelaire, *Selected Writings on Art and Literature*, trans. P. E. Charvet (Penguin, 2006), chapter 13. For a recent study of Nietzsche on Wagner, see Ryan Harvey and Aaron Ridley, *Nietzsche's The Case of Wagner and Nietzsche contra Wagner* (Edinburgh: Edinburgh University Press, 2022). Although they provide valuable insights into Nietzsche on Wagner's music and decadence, the authors do not touch on the link Nietzsche makes between the content of Wagner's art and the literary work of "Parisian decadents." In his notebooks of 1888, Nietzsche characterises several "modern pessimists" as decadents, including Schopenhauer, Leopardi, Baudelaire, and Dostoyevsky (*KSA* 13, 14 [222] and 15 [34]). For details on Nietzsche's reception of Baudelaire, see Karl Pestalozzi, "Nietzsche's Baudelaire-Rezeption," Nietzsche-Studien 7 (1978): 158–78. Richard Sieburth, "Introduction," in Charles Baudelaire, *Late Fragments,* trans. Richard Sieburth (Yale University Press, 2022), 60–66.

51 KSA 11, 38 [5], 160. Compare Paul Bourget, "The Example of Baudelaire," trans. Nancy O' Connor, *New England Review* 30, no. 2 (2009): 90–104.

52 KSA 13, 14 [47]; WP 821.

53 KSA 13, 11 [312], 132; WP 849.

54 KSA 12, 2 [114]; WP 845.

55 WP 846; see also GS 370.

56 Baudelaire, *Selected Writings*, 188. See also note 18. In the letter to Gast I refer to, it is evident that Nietzsche had some knowledge of Baudelaire's views on decadence.

57 Baudelaire, *Selected Writings*, 188, 189. See also the poem "Elevation" from the "Spleen and the Ideal," part of Baudelaire's *The Flowers of Evil*, trans. James McGowan (Oxford University Press, 1993), 17.

58 Benjamin, *Selected Writings*, 135.

59 Benjamin, 147.

60 Benjamin, 154.

61 See Roger Pearson, *The Beauty of Baudelaire: The Poet as Alternative Lawgiver* (Oxford University Press, 2021), especially part two, for a recent and extensive analysis of Baudelaire on melancholy. Pearson rightly notes that Baudelaire understands "le Mal"—presented not as Christian evil but rather as secular ill-being—as a condition of melancholy synonymous with the human business of living.

62 GS 125.
63 GS 343.
64 Leo Bersani, *Baudelaire and Freud* (University of California Press, 1977),140.
65 Baudelaire, *Selected Writings*, 419.
66 Baudelaire, 421. See Benjamin, *The Writer of Modern Life: Essays on Baudelaire*, ed. Michael W. Jennings (Harvard University Press, 2006), 124. Rainer Hanshe has recently, and intelligently, sought to save Baudelaire's aristocratic conception of a noble, self-cultivating dandyism from the populism of the fop and capitalist pop star of our own time, where self-fashioning is reduced to a mere matter of style or an attitudinal pose. Hanshe rightly observes that this is nothing other than conformism to the culture of capitalism. Rainer J. Hanshe, "Introduction," in Charles Baudelaire, *My Heart Laid Bare & Other Texts*, trans. Rainer J. Hanshe (Contra Mundum Press, 2020), xviii-xix. Interestingly, he notes the influence of Emerson on Baudelaire and his citing from Emerson's *The Conduct of Life*: "Great men . . . have not been boasters or buffoons, but perceivers of the *terror of life*, and have manned themselves to face it." Baudelaire, *My Heart Laid Bare & Other Texts*, 62. Baudelaire is citing from the beginning of the essay on "Fate" that opens Emerson's *The Conduct of Life* (Harvard University Press, 2003), 2. He omits from the sentence that he cites Emerson's reference to "great nations" as well as "great men."
67 Baudelaire, *Selected Writings*, 420.
68 Baudelaire, 421. See also Baudelaire, 259: "To be aristocratic is to be isolated."
69 Baudelaire, 422.
70 Baudelaire, 419.
71 Z II, "On the Famous Wise Men."
72 GS 283.
73 GS 283.
74 Z III: "Of Old and New Law-Tables," 14.
75 NCW, "We Antipodes."
76 D 549; see also the criticism in D 50 on "belief in intoxication."
77 KSA 11, 25 [164]; SUP 15, 48.
78 KSA 11, 25 [164]; SUP 15, 48.
79 KSA 11, 25 [181]; 53. Henry James was a perceptive critic of Flaubert's hatred of bourgeois life, noting how it distorted his view of the world and impaired him as an artist. See chapters 16 and 49 of Henry James, *The Critical Muse: Selected Literary Criticism*, ed. Roger Gard (Penguin, 1987), 96–103 and 373–403.
80 KSA 11, 25 [216]; 60; see also 26 [458], 252; and BGE 218, TI, "Maxims and Barbs," 34 and CW, 9.
81 KSA 11, 25 [164]; SUP 15, 48.
82 D 442.
83 Koenraad W. Swart, *The Sense of Decadence in Nineteenth-Century France* (Martinus Nijhoff, 1964) provides valuable insight into modern French writers and authors and their relation to Romantic idealism and decadence. He argues that while Flaubert sought

to illustrate the dangers of Romantic idealism in his novels—for example, in *Madame Bovary* and *Sentimental Education*—he belonged to a group of self-styled realists who did not fully overcome Romanticism, and who admitted themselves that they suffered from the nervous exhaustion and irritability of a decadent era: Swart, 112. Baudelaire, he suggests, "betrayed a conventional nostalgia for the lost virtues of the past": Swart, 114. Valéry's views on the romantics, and on Baudelaire's relation to Romanticism, are also well worth considering. Paul Valéry, *Leonardo, Poe, Mallarmé*, trans. Malcolm Cowley and James R. Lawler (Routledge and Kegan Paul, 1972), 193–215, especially 196–198 and 200–202. As he points out, Romanticism needs to be treated as something of an arbitrary idea. Nietzsche stands out, though, as a thinker and writer dedicated to a poetry and a philosophy of the future and the heralding of new virtues and a new goal for humanity.

84 Christopher Isherwood, *Exhumations* (Harmondsworth: Penguin, 1969), 41. On Baudelaire and the city, see chapters 18 and 19 of Pearson, *The Beauty of Baudelaire*, and the study by Ross Chambers, *An Atmospherics of the City: Baudelaire and the Poetics of Noise* (Fordham University Press, 2015).

85 KSA 11, 25 [164]; SUP 15, 48.

86 CW 1. One facet of Turin that delighted Nietzsche when he took up residence there in 1888 was that he found it "Not at all a metropolis, not at all modern . . ." Letter to Peter Gast in Christopher Middleton, *Selected Letters of Friedrich Nietzsche* (Hackett, 1996), 291.

87 EH, Foreword, 3.

88 Baudelaire, "Further Notes on Edgar Poe," in *Selected Writings*, 197.

89 Pearson, *The Beauty of Baudelaire*, xi.

90 Baudelaire, *Selected Writings*, 268 (my emphasis).

We Have Ways of Making You Talk: Parsing Nietzsche's Philology

Jason Barker and Justin Clemens

We Have Ways of Making You Talk

Friedrich Nietzsche says it himself. *Pathos* is elementary: it is will to power. It precedes being and becoming, no matter what fumble-fingered philosophers have hitherto tried to make of them. Being and becoming proceed from pathos.[1] Pathos is indiscernible, having no predicates to distinguish it from its own differences, but it is also imperceptible, not just because it cannot be directly perceived at all, but also insofar as it is only itself by not being itself. The apparently identical may be antithetical; the imperceptible must be non-identical. This is why Alain Badiou claims, contra Gilles Deleuze, that "Nietzsche's last word is not sense, but the unevaluable."[2] Is then pathos the *archē*, an *archē*, or an *an-archē*? Nietzsche notoriously calls for "a revaluation of all values." All values are necessarily revaluable, being interpretations; every interpretation is already multiple, given that it only persists in being-repeated; in being-repeated, it necessarily differs from itself, if only numerically; yet even this mere numerical differentiation threatens to turn zeros into twos and teens through the indecent aggregation of placeholders. Divergence is the *archē* of the *archē*, commencement and commandment as immediate recommencement and dissent, the grand spasm of an insensible inauguration.

Pathos is thus the great educator, and all educators—even great ones—are hence necessarily pathetic. Still, this hardly equalises them—quite to the contrary. Yet there must be education; indeed, there must be *re*-education. How to do it? The question is complicated by the fact that the educational system of Nietzsche's day is not just necessarily pathetic. In January 1872, the Extraordinary Professor of Classical Philology would begin his Basel lecture series on the future of education and publish *The Birth of Tragedy*. And yet as he would come to realise in his "Attempt at Self-Criticism," education is but the symptom of a culture in terminal decline. In fact, far from inspiring the overhaul of the educational system, all that Germany's democratic modernity qua mediocrity is able to inspire in Nietzsche—beyond the diagnosis of nihilism itself—are bouts of uncontrollable Dionysian laughter and derision.[3]

Nietzsche, we know, is the pioneer of the no-less-abominable torments of *self*-education, long since incorporated into the postmodern Ponzi schemes of agonistic self-improvement. Perhaps it would have been preferable simply to abandon or destroy our educational institutions altogether, at least for the sake of putting future generations of mass students out of their misery. But wouldn't such academic iconoclasm constitute an ur- (an über!-) educational act in itself? Perhaps the final Nietzschean solution is to confine "education" to the aristocratic realm in which art and science comprise purely aesthetic phenomena to be lived, one where "genius" has sufficient scope for its praxis, and lesser minds the good sense not to get involved.[4]

In an address to students, the nineteenth-century Anglo-Irish physicist John Tyndall speaks of how the mental gymnastics required to parse grammatically wayward English sentences can prove a valuable training ground for the scientific imagination. Tyndall writes:

> The piercing through the involved and inverted sentences of *Paradise Lost*; the linking of the verb to its often distant nominative, of the relative to its distant antecedent, of the agent to the object of the transitive verb, of the preposition to the noun or pronoun which it governed, the study of variations in mood and tense, the transpositions often necessary to bring out the true grammatical structure of a sentence—all this was to my young mind a discipline of the highest value, and a source of unflagging delight. How I rejoiced when I found a great author tripping, and was fairly able to pin him to a corner from which there was no escape! As I speak, some of the sentences which exercised me when a boy rise to my recollection. For instance, "He that hath ears to hear, let him hear"; where the "He" is left, as it were, floating in mid air without any verb to support it.[5]

Tyndall's contemporaneous fame derived from his studies of magnetism and crystallography, if his abiding import today perhaps depends on his work on thermal radiation, including experimental confirmation in 1859 of the greenhouse effect.

His pertinence in this context comes from his account of childhood reading as constituting a knot of education, grammar, and God, which delivers both discipline and delight as a condition for a scientific orientation to the world.

Tyndall gives two examples: first, John Milton's *Paradise Lost*, the greatest English epic poem; second, a verbatim citation of the phrase from Matthew 11.15, "He that hath ears to hear, let him hear." Epic poetry and the Bible: Tyndall's instances are not only canonical, but self-reflexive. They index a key organ of sense that makes sense of the initially senseless or nonsensical. Here it's the ear: the ineluctable modality of the audible, as James Joyce might say. But it is also the case that the ear enters through the reading eye—perhaps as a camel through a needle—hearing and seeing together, if not entirely reconciled, transmitted by letters, by alphabets; yet it also alludes to an acoustic event, a transformation that bypasses visible letters altogether, or, rather, that maintains that letters only transcribe events through dissimulation.

For Tyndall, education is an auto-education in the effective materials of the insensible through a piercing linguistic analysis of grammatical functions in their apparent contravention. It is also so as a form of competition or *agon*, the reader essaying to adjudge the possible or actual legitimacy or error of the writer's disruptions. To put this yet another way: interiorisation is a discipline generated by means of a struggle for sense, qua the open secret of syntax out of the unsensible sensations of presentation. Yet such discipline also entails a certain forgetting that ought to be recalled (perhaps like a corporate product recall): that the very clarity and order of organs in their apparent concert are the result of long-suffering, structuring, and submission.

Given we are allegedly speaking here in a Nietzschean fashion of the pathetic spasms that are the unfigurable archetypes of the metamorphoses of the human, we are confronted by a kind of historical or even genealogical enigma machine whose assembly and strata of assemblages are in question. In the face of what Kostas Axelos terms "the great powers and the elementary forces of the world,"[6] what are the switching points or signatures of this scientific self-education by singular syntaxes? For example, how to reconstruct from Tyndall's account of his auto-educative reorganisation of his organs a genealogy, archaeology, or even geology of the dissimulating echoes of more primal spasms?

We know that education is at the heart of Nietzsche's project; or, more precisely, the question of re-education. Whether he is speaking of Homer or Wagner, Greek tragedy or troubadours, the motif of education recurs throughout his oeuvre—and not least because this oeuvre is littered with love letters to his own self-professed educators that he will later bitterly renounce.[7] What remains consistent is the conviction that all true education proceeds affectively, through disturbances; that is, by *pathos*. The morass of what is misnamed "education" must be affected by the event of a true educator. As Nietzsche puts it in his *Unfashionable Observations* on Schopenhauer, titled precisely "Schopenhauer as Educator":

> What is amazing here is how in the service of a fundamentally extrahuman and suprahuman enterprise—pure, inconsequential, and hence passionless knowledge—a host of very human drives and petty passions have been mixed together to form a chemical compound, and how the result, the scholar, appears so transfigured in the light of that supraterrestrial, lofty, and thoroughly pure enterprise, that one completely forgets the measuring and mixing that was necessary in order to produce him in the first place.[8]

The very *unfruitfulness* of this particular mode of measuring and mixing means "the epitaph of university philosophy should read: 'It never disturbed anyone.'"[9] *Hear, hear!* as they used to say, although there may still be the troubling whisper of a paradox, given the scholar remains a world-historical achievement for Nietzsche, the unprecedented production of unnatural passionless purity. In *On the Future of Our Educational Institutions*, he provides a staggering image of the organisation of transmission:

> If a foreigner desires to know something of the methods of our universities, he asks first of all with emphasis: "How is the student connected with the university?" We answer: "By the ear, as a hearer." The foreigner is astonished. "Only by the ear?" he repeats. "Only by the ear," we again reply. The student hears . . . The student very often writes down something while he hears; and it is only at these rare moments that he hangs on the umbilical cord of his alma mater . . . One speaking mouth, with many ears, and half as many writing hands—there you have to all appearances, the external academical apparatus; the university engine of culture set in motion.[10]

Such state-sponsored networks of part-organs will repeat through Nietzsche's writing life—take the famous image of the giant ear of the inverse cripple from Zarathustra—perhaps to be summarised in later works as the type of the "last men," those who do not boast that they live, but that they survive—and then "blink and cough." Unlike the legislators of the future, the last men are so educated as to be entirely ineducable.[11]

So, we shouldn't forget that Nietzsche himself began as a scholar, a remarkable one, and we should perhaps therefore credit him with knowing what he is talking about. Or perhaps not. In any case, he was not just any kind of scholar, bound to the ancient state institution of the university—itself with an august history stemming back to Barbarossa's stunning inauguration of a new conceptual war-machine directed against the Church—but the very model of a major modern scholar, the German philologist. As Laurence Lampert puts it: "To suppose that Nietzsche had no training in a scientific discipline is false: he was acknowledged the most promising man of his generation in the discipline of philology."[12] And philology (lest we forget!) was—and is—a science, a real science, a rigorous science of letters, of their emergence, deployment, and metamorphosis over vast tracts of time and space.

Yet, as Elie During also reminds us, "Philology is at bottom nothing but an art (or science) of hypotheses. One of its most essential tools (at least in Nietzsche's time) is the so-called critical or conjectural method, which consists in filling the gaps in a text or a doctrine by devising conjectures."[13] In order to have value, that is, revalue values, such conjectures or speculations must metastasise the missing moments of mutilated monuments—we might even say as in the art of the dream, insofar as Nietzsche holds in *The Dionysian Vision of the World* (1870, a draft that immediately precedes *The Birth of Tragedy*) that, if dreams are plays with actuality, the maker of art plays with the dream itself.[14] Dionysius as the speculative reconstruction of what's not, no longer, was never there: will to power. Not a description, but a legislation; not a reformation, but the unleashing of inexistent chaos in reforming it for new kinds of life.

In fact, there is something to be said for modernity itself being a philological dream, a dream of philology, but possibly also of philology as the art of the dream. Hannah Arendt notes in *The Human Condition* that:

> Three great events stand at the threshold of the modern age and determine its character: the discovery of America and the ensuing exploration of the whole earth; the Reformation, which by expropriating ecclesiastical and monastic possessions started the two-fold process of individual expropriation and the accumulation of social wealth; the invention of the telescope and the development of a new science that considers the nature of the earth from the viewpoint of the universe.[15]

If we can take Arendt's remark as a reasonable orientation to the problematic, let's propose that modern history, that is, the becoming of European capitalism as a world system, that is, the regime of philology, cannot be separated from colonialism nor the Reformation nor Galilean science. If philology was already a hallmark of what we still call the early Renaissance, it was given a decisive impetus by the encounter with non-European scripts from China to Peru, the enigmatic characters of glyphs, graphemes, and other grams, an emergent discipline at once hyperconscious of the Babelian inheritance of mutually incomprehensible languages *and* concerned with their lost roots, their becoming and their potential universality.

It accompanies and undertakes the reclamation of ancient texts, their editing, translation, and republication, as well as drawing from the esoteric power traditions of magic and cryptography, kabbalah, and criticism.

Indeed, philology is at the root of the Protestant Reformation. As Walter Benjamin famously remarked, Luther's translation of the Bible into the vernacular is the decisive event of the modern German language itself. Phenomenology may have proclaimed that it was going back to the things themselves, but in this it was downstream of the Reformation which returned to the sacred texts themselves, in an effort to cleanse them of the encrustations of secular power, that is, of the covering-over by lacks. Arendt herself somewhere remarks that all the great German philosophers from Leibniz until Heidegger were Protestants. Philologically speaking, we also know, in Jean-Luc Nancy's provocative phrase, that the Germans read Greek particularly well.

As for science, it is itself dependent on this revolution of the letter in the wake of colonial rapacity and reforming zealotry. In Jean-Claude Milner's account:

> According to Alexandre Koyré, a radical shift occurred when Galileo used mathematics to calculate not only celestial phenomena, but also those of the sublunary world. . . . Galileo summed up this decision in a formula: the book of the universe is written in mathematical letters. But let us take another look at this formula. For Koyré, the important word is *mathematics*. For me, the important word is *letters*. In my opinion, what defines Galilean science is this *literalization*.[16]

Moreover, as Milner proceeds to underline, Galileo "believed that philology should serve as the model for physics much as philology was at that moment the pioneer in the deciphering and correction of written texts."[17] It is hence the power of the philologised letter that proves the decisive philtre for modern physics.

Yet, if we can say that philology binds this triple knot of rapacious colonialism, Reformed Christianity, and revolutionary science, we would also have to say that this act of binding transforms philology itself. Once again, since we are trying to be good Nietzscheans here, the task would be to *cherchez le pathétique*! Here's Werner Hamacher ranting on the very topic:

> The Christianity of philology took an embarrassing turn with its reform in the sixteenth century, which to this day has not ceased in its effects. The divine *logos* of John the Evangelist, at one with love, became a God that hated creation and condemned his believers to spend their lives in *hatred of self* (Luther, "95 Theses," no. 4). The most pitiless consciousness of guilt is thus imputed by a word, a language, a discourse that represents the simple perversion of the *logos* that was still in force in the *philia* of Plato and John. What is said in the phrase, *hatred for oneself* is: language hates us, condemns us, persecutes us, and we hate, condemn, and persecute ourself and, in ourselves, language whenever we seek to make ourselves understood in it and about it. (—*Was heißt, haßt.*—).[18]

Perhaps then it's no surprise that Nietzsche himself began his career as a self-loathing imperialist Lutheran philologist, a prodigious one—if he ended as none of them.[19]

The Birth of Tragedy is already concerned with reconstructing the dance of letters, the struggle between ear and eye, mouth and feet, sound and image. Socrates, who does not write, is the decadence of the—all-singing, all-dancing, all-declaiming—masked tragedy, which has to pass through writing to achieve its immortal transience in the very loss of its artistic character.

Cupid and Psyche

Is philology decadent? Do its classical pretensions to the myth of Greek serenity drive it headlong into the underworld? Or, alternatively, does its power reside in an art or science of classical restoration that "we philologists" are duty-bound to pursue, albeit in an educational landscape profoundly ill-suited to achieving this end? This opposition is misleading. (It is, of course, no secret that Nietzsche will often find himself running in neither direction at once). First, as an early-career scholar, Nietzsche was prone to take his cues from Schopenhauer in matters of education and Kant in matters of art. Both advocated moral dispensations and aesthetic detachments which Nietzsche, once retired from Basel University and estranged from Wagner, would find organically repulsive. The pathos would become not just disturbing, but also convulsive. In short, he would suffer hallucinations his entire adult life. However, in *The Birth of Tragedy*, philology remains part and parcel of Nietzsche's constitutionally restorative manifesto on education—even if the accepted discursive form of its presentation is conspicuous by its absence, if not downright hallucinatory.

Nietzsche's university friend, the classicist Erwin Rohde, will acknowledge this lack in his reply to the book's harshest critic, Ulrich von Wilamowitz-Moellendorff, the philologist—himself at the time unknown—who, paradoxically, despite inveighing against Nietzsche's scandalous flouting of scientific method, litters his own "critique" with misquotations, and has to resort to self-publishing his invective in pamphlet form, since no academic journal would carry it.[20]

In his *Afterphilologie*—the ironically titled rejoinder to Wilamowitz's *Zukunftsphilologie!*—Rohde mounts his counterattack by reading Nietzsche's text *as if* it were possessed of the philological architecture—the *Fußnotenphilologie*—that it so conspicuously lacked. Suddenly, the footnotes "returned," courtesy of Rohde's bottom-heavy text, like an alter-ego: *iacet corpus dormientis ut mortui, viget autem et vivit animus.*[21] Might we say that this *psychic* undertaking—a so-apposite symptomatic reading by Rohde, who would become the nineteenth century's foremost expert in the science of the Greek soul—intends for its scientific aim the unfashionable *resurrection* of Nietzsche's *Fußnotenphilologie?* Surely nothing could be more un-Greek! For we know that once dead souls cross the river to reach Hades, they never come back alive. And yet they continue to live—albeit invisibly—below.

Literally, what do Rohde's scholarly mind games consist of? According to James I. Porter,

> In short, [Rohde] wished to prove that Nietzsche's book presupposed conventional philological knowledge and then shifted the arguments to a higher level, one that took in the problems of culture, religion, philosophy, and the very nature of the discipline of classics. In the process, it deliberately eschewed the form of a primer or, as he repeatedly dubbed it, a "*Hülfsbuchlein*" (brief handbook). Meanwhile, Wilamowitz, Rohde argued, was set on reducing the problems to just such a level, namely, that of an undergraduate survey. Rohde effectively depicted Wilamowitz as an overeager secondary schooler, fresh out of Schulpforta, who wanted to counter Nietzsche with the sort of erudition that could be found in any handbook and who sought to bolster his case with a mountain of citations from antiquity. At turns patient and exasperated, Rohde, still twenty-six years old and three years Wilamowitz's senior, tried to give the newly minted Ph.D., whom he variously addressed as "the Dr. phil." and "the pamphleteer" or "the diatribist [der Pasquillant]," a lesson in "the philology of the present and the future."[22]

Wilamowitz must have been equally hard of hearing to have missed the spirit of music emanating from Nietzsche's text. Although, to be fair to the pedant, and as Nietzsche will remark many years later (no doubt with Wilamowitz in mind): "where a book tells only of experiences which it is quite impossible to have often or even just rarely . . . simply nothing will be heard, with the acoustic illusion that where nothing is heard *nothing is there, either.*"[23]

Might the curious case of *The Birth of Tragedy's* prophetic (i.e., missing) footnotes evince a covert strategy that Nietzsche would eventually (and unsuccessfully) back away from? A covert philology? "We Philologists," the fifth essay of the planned thirteen *Unfashionable Observations* (withheld from publication in 1876) would appear posthumously. In it, we find a master plan for education that its author apparently found too futuristic by halves: "In short, ninety-nine philologists out of a hundred *should* not be philologists at all."[24] There are no "disinterested philologists," laments Nietzsche, which requires that we "secure for philology the universally educative results which it should bring about":[25]

> The means: the limitation of the number of those engaged in the philological profession (doubtful whether young men should be made acquainted with philology at all). Criticism of the philologist. The value of antiquity: It sinks with you: how deeply you must have sunk, since its value is now so little![26]

Observe how, in 1874, two years following *The Birth of Tragedy*'s publication, Nietzsche is hardly practising Dionysian gymnastics—not even in private. Perhaps the Wilamowitz-Nietzsche controversy (in which Richard Wagner was a central protagonist: Rohde's pamphlet was in fact an open letter to the latter) hadn't so much been lived down as absorbed into the greater whole. Whatever qualms its author may have had about its publication, "We Philologists" by no means reads as a career suicide note. A more prosaic and level-headed interpretation of why the manuscript never emerged as an *Unfashionable Observation* is surely boredom. "Disinterested philology" or "disinterested education" appears to have won the day here: "The value of antiquity: it sinks with you." Ever more reason to curtail the number of philologists! Superior ones, certainly. Geniuses, perhaps.

In his letter of 16 July 1872 to Rohde—in which the royal prerogative prevails—one encounters the literary Führer not merely dictating the content of Rohde's reply to Wilamowitz, but *type-setting the manuscript* for him. As Nietzsche will inform Rohde, in an act of Machiavellian ventriloquism that would have made the English football manager Brian Clough blush:

> Here, my dear good friend, is the title [of your pamphlet], discovered amid rejoicing and shrieks of derision by my fellow lodger Professor Overbeck.

> Dr. U. Wilamowitz-Moellendorf's
> *Afterphilologie*
> Open Letter
> to Richard Wagner
> by a Philologist
>
> You can then put your own name under the letter, at the end (but in full and with all titles!). In the conclusion you can placidly address Wilamowitz as an "Afterphilolog." For us he represents a "false" philology, and the success of your piece will be to show him as such to others.[27]

The value of antiquity sinks with "you," indeed. Rohde would refrain from signing the pamphlet, although the attempt to let "disinterested philology" prevail didn't prevent Wilamowitz from being "privy to the rumor mill"[28] and unmasking the *hypokritēs*. The rest of Nietzsche's letter to Rohde, ventriloquism aside, stands as decisive proof of "their" argument; namely, that *The Birth of Tragedy* wasn't so much "lacking" in footnotes; on the contrary, the author's references were *glaringly obvious* to any halfway-decent undergraduate (cynics might retort: an inverse cripple with a giant eye to find them). Wasn't that the type of reader that Nietzsche—or any self-respecting author—was duty-bound to write for, even if it wasn't exactly the one he was searching for? Why patronise one's readership with common sense? As Nietzsche will confirm to Rohde, Wilamowitz is philologically mistaken on so many points, notably the misconstrual of Nietzsche's mention of "goat-legged" satyrs. Despite his admittedly "offensive" choice of terms, the "theory about the satyrs" advanced by Nietzsche was "of great importance" and "something essentially new." When Nietzsche talks about the "field of inquiry" pertaining to his discoveries, we can assume he does in fact mean philology.[29] His letter to Rohde will proceed to sketch out primary and secondary sources, ancient and modern, in support of his satyr theory.[30]

So, *The Birth of Tragedy* can be depicted in many ways, except, perhaps above all, as the *anti-philology* that might suit the agendas of Nietzsche's various detractors and supporters. James I. Porter draws attention, in his *Nietzsche and the Philology of the Future*, to the ignorance among contemporary scholars of the relationship between philosophy and philology in its nineteenth-century German academic context.[31] Such ignorance may help to explain the subsequent fashion in Nietzschean anti-philosophy and all things Nietzsche. As for Nietzsche's contemporary assassins, they too, Porter reveals, were equally misguided. Aside from Wilamowitz, Hermann Usener, with whom Nietzsche had planned to publish "a complete reappraisal of the history of ancient philosophy,"[32] will publicly take aim at the author of *The Birth of Tragedy* in the year of its publication, bluntly proclaiming him "dead to scholarship."[33]

Nothing in Nietzsche's professional biography suggests that the description was inaccurate or that Usener had failed to hit the bullseye, though perhaps not in the manner intended.[34] Needless to say, Nietzsche wasn't remotely stung by it, as a separate letter to Rohde indicates.[35] That Nietzsche was professionally engaged in the Homeric Hades of philology also goes without saying, to the extent that such bitter accusations are simply planks in his theoretical edifice, or the wreckage he endeavours to salvage as it washes ashore.

And yet the psychic level on which Nietzsche is operating may certainly frustrate a neatly dialectical reading of *The Birth of Tragedy*, according to which the negation of philology subsists, or its parts return to overwhelm the philosopher, who fails to escape philology even in retirement. It's difficult to read Nietzsche's permanent wandering ministry, from the Mediterranean coast to the Engadine Alps, his constant back and forth with the changing seasons, as anything other than a kind of literary purgatory; albeit, strictly speaking, a *Homeric* sorting-office of letters, with nothing in the way of celestial relief. However, let us focus on the literary *method*, not the wandering per se: the philological sceptic rather than the philosopher of the meandering poetic imagination.

"We Philologists" is not the only bold statement in Nietzsche's relentless search for a method. In *Homer and Classical Philology,* his inaugural Basel University speech of 28 May 1869, we find the young Nietzsche operating once more on the psychic level, summoning the vanished spirits of the One who would be named Homer. Or "Homer." Needless to say, Nietzsche could be talking about himself here, and the Wilamowitzian philistinism that lay just over the horizon:

> Since literary history first ceased to be a mere collection of names, people have attempted to grasp and formulate the individualities of the poets. A certain mechanism forms part of the method: it must be explained—*i.e.*, it must be deduced from principles—why this or that individuality appears in this way and not in that. People now study biographical details, environment, acquaintances, contemporary events, and believe that by mixing all these ingredients together they will be able to manufacture the wished-for individuality. But they forget that the *punctum saliens*, the indefinable individual characteristics, can never be obtained from a compound of this nature.[36]

The "individuality" of the work, its coherence, does not rely on the mixing of ingredients. "Homer" isn't a matter of the formulas—the "historical tradition" handed down from antiquity—that the half-decent undergraduate should know by heart. Instead, "Homer" is "an *aesthetic judgement*,"[37] which sounds a thoroughly un-Nietzschean sort of statement, given the deep-rooted anti-historicism of much of Nietzsche's own writing. Might it be read as yet another instance of Nietzsche's untimely critique, where in exposing the poet's "individuality" he exposes the classical pretensions of authorship per se, and with it his own? The author is dead, and so too the speaking subject, "Nietzsche."

This is not the place to get into the sort of labyrinthine dialectics such aporias throw up, as if they hadn't already been rehearsed enough. Critical philology in Nietzsche's hands is far too serious a discipline to see its significance in untimely, unfashionable, and frankly unwelcome critique, the conceptual dynamite for shaking up a decadent institution. Witness in what James I. Porter describes as Nietzsche's "sceptical philology" a form of classical doxography in extremis.[38] In Porter's depiction, the young Nietzsche is by turns customs inspector, art detective, and even the laboratory forensics expert ready to run ink tests on suspected forgeries. Will it all come down to things in themselves? Antique reconstruction didn't sit well with Nietzsche's obsessive personality. Mercifully (for him), he wouldn't live to see the computing age. His letters provide not just ample material for parsing—the *pars orationis* of that "individuality"—they equally contain countless examples of actual computing machines or what's more commonly known today as software applications or "apps."

One can barely avoid reading Nietzsche's epigrams and aphorisms, letters, and fragmentary notes as sets of "random" data strings.[39] The recursive word association games of a dilettante inspire, in turn, the recursive word association games of dilettantes, and so on *ad infinitum*. And yet the "Letters of Insanity," to take one of countless examples—which include the proper names: Isoline, Dionysus, Wilhelm, Buddha, Caesar, Caiaphas, Ariadne, Shakespeare, the Crucified . . . —are *determinate* data strings that can be parsed to *decide* valid grammatical expressions of the Nietzsche lexicon. For example, one could imagine ordering any expression from the "Letters" by 1) proper name, 2) pseudonym, 3) both, or 4) neither (one might wish to include significant crossings out of the ~~Caesar~~ type).

Nietzsche appears to admit the technique in his retrospective remarks on *The Birth of Tragedy*. In what follows, he could be imagining the "find and replace" function of the word processor. Here the psychologist and the philologist come together in one profession:

> A psychologist might add that what I heard in Wagnerian music in my youth has nothing whatsoever to do with Wagner; that when I was describing Dionysian music I was describing what *I* had heard—that I instinctively had

> to translate and transfigure everything into the new spirit I bore inside me. The proof of this, *as strong a proof as any can be*, is my work *Wagner in Bayreuth*: in all the psychologically decisive passages it speaks of me alone—one can ruthlessly put my name or the word "Zarathustra" wherever the text has the word "Wagner."[40]

Such indifferent literary stock-taking sits uncomfortably on the hallowed terrain of classical philology with its consideration of the sacred texts themselves. And yet one can hardly discount it from "future philology" for any number of reasons. Aren't philologists ultimately concerned with obtaining the *strongest possible proofs*? Nietzsche's sceptical philology first comes to light in his project to collect the fragments of the Greek atomist Democritus of Abdera, which he began in the summer of 1867. Nietzsche would never bring the project to completion. However, through stages it would assume "an entirely inexhaustible character,"[41] and remain a nagging obsession until his retirement from Basel University in 1879. Nietzsche demands exactitude on the question of whether X title of Democritus can or cannot be authenticated of the "yes," "no," or "maybe" variety. His model philologist, we learn, was Valentin Rose, something of a no-nonsense, fraud squad-style specialist in impounding ghost writings (his *Aristoteles Pseudepigraphus* [1863] has since fallen into disrepute[42]). There was literally no fragment small enough that Rose wasn't prepared to cast into the infinite void of doubt.

Those inclined to see this obsessive and somewhat unhinged approach as "reductive" would be well advised to reconsider the hallowed terrain of classical philology and its transmission of sacred texts. There is no reason to think that the irreducible complexity of a literary work is somehow stymied or diminished through computational parsing. Indeed, ultimately, as Gregory Chaitin proves, "irreducible complexity" is algorithmically random, which is to say *computationally incompressible*.[43] Today, enmeshed in the artificial neural networks of Google Search, ChatGPT, and emergent large language models, literary analysis and its object—the science of letters—have become really indistinguishable, if not identical, in literary terms. Moreover, name the contemporary scholar, or anyone at all, whose entire life isn't a mere routine of network computing. To say that "Democritus is the paradox of Nietzsche's philology, and inseparable from his conception of him"[44] suggests that Nietzsche's "method," much like the "man himself," is algorithmic, or inexhaustibly mimetic, running with no precise purpose other than precision itself, precision being that gram of pathos which synchronises his writing like a Kantian timepiece. "Nietzsche's punctuation in his letters tended to be idiosyncratic"[45] is one way of putting it. The sceptical philologist has ways of making you talk.

Geniuses of All Lands, Unite! You Have Everything to Lose But Your Slaves!

We have set anchor on the far-from-hallowed shores of modern education, where philology and philosophy departments still strive to find the right readers, whether by fishhook, neural nets, or more intelligent means. In truth, nothing is remotely left to chance in the modern university, while "disinterested education" has been banished to the University of Life. Nietzsche would have surely approved.

In *Nietzsche, The Aristocratic Rebel*, Domenico Losurdo presents us with a counterfactual history of the world, of Western culture and civilisation in toto, from the ancient Greeks to the industrial age, seen through the dark shades of Nietzsche's appalling vision.[46] Epic chapter titles like "Manifesto of the Party of the Tragic View of the World" and "The 'Doric State' as Dictatorship in the Service of the Production of Genius" provide the general idea of a Hegel *turned back on his head*. Imagine living in a world, as Nietzsche cannot help but do in his pathetic outpourings to Rohde, where the communards had *actually won*. Of course, had they won, then titles of the aforementioned variety would no longer have the satirical ring of George Orwell novels. Which begs the question of precisely *which* world Nietzsche's educational manifestos are most suited to: decadent democracy, where socialists swarm like fetid dwarves? Or restoration aristocracy, where the slaves are kept conveniently out of sight?

In the fifth and final lecture of *On the Future of Our Educational Institutions*, delivered on 23 March 1872, Nietzsche's Socratic dialogue reaches the point where our learned protagonist has to decide what that future is going to be. From our perspective, the "educational debate" is less a case of standing in judgement on the future direction of western culture and civilisation, and more about whether the alienated stakeholder will be able to afford any education at all. No doubt this is precisely the "divide" (between bourgeois and proletarians) that Nietzsche anticipates, and is endeavouring, in his own "semi-aristocratic" class interests, to ward off. But what Nietzsche may not entirely understand—it may be an article of his faith—is that while the classes themselves are fixed, the point of the divide separating them (*all* "division" for the communists) certainly is not.

The confusion is perhaps most evident when Nietzsche expresses the view that "the present type of university [is] a mere appendage to the public school":

> Do not, then, let yourselves be deceived in regard to the cultured student; for he, insofar as he thinks he has absorbed the blessings of education, is merely the public school boy as moulded by the hands of his teacher: one who, since his academical isolation, and after he has left the public school, has therefore been deprived of all further guidance to culture, that from now on he may begin to live by himself and be free.[47]

He that hath ears to hear, let him hear! And yet some ears are bigger than others. The problem of finding one's readership or knowing who to write for is rather like recruiting the right students. While the halfway-decent undergraduate—he who, in Nietzsche's view, is a mere function of the public school—may not be so bright in the company of Cambridge scholars, the same student would certainly outshine a class of high school dropouts. And the difficulty in determining academic "standards" becomes somewhat more complicated when the institution in question is to specialise in the cultivation of genius, which is not something which can actually be learned or taught. Since genius is a natural aptitude, the only business the genius has being in school, Kant informs us, is to produce exemplary models of genius, which may be imitated, although the genius "does not himself know how the ideas for it come to him, and also does not have it in his power to think up such things at will or according to plan, and to communicate to others precepts that would put them in a position to produce similar products."[48]

The genius is something of a blockhead, then. He can't help it. And don't expect him to tell you what he's doing, because he doesn't know. And even if he *did* know, he wouldn't be able to tell you, at least not in a way that would make any sense.[49] Kant himself, oddly enough, accepts there to be "original nonsense" whose "products must at the same time be models."[50] One is reminded of the scene in *This Is Spinal Tap!* in which the documentary filmmaker endeavours to prise from the mercurial guitarist the secrets of his creative process, only to be told not to touch, point, or even look at his guitar. Art as a unifying of all the nonsenses? Such geniuses needn't be ashamed. Homer didn't know what he was doing, either. Or that he was Homer. The Homer question is one for philology. In fact, is it not the case that the real genius, in Nietzsche's estimation, is the philologist whose *aesthetic judgement* is responsible for creating Homer? Clearly not, for "Homer" must be the original, supplying models for imitation, and thus setting the standard for all art, "*i.e.*, as a standard or rule of estimating."[51]

For Nietzsche himself, education "is first and foremost obedience and submission to the discipline of genius."[52] And yet the institutional framework for enacting discipline—along with the reproduction of the "hierarchy of spirits"—is lamentably absent. One just can't get the staff these days. In his ruminations on the idea of the ideal university, Nietzsche is struck by the uneasy relationship between philosophers, or the higher artists and free spirits, and philologists, which he characterises without compunction as philosophy's industrious handmaidens:

> It has thus come to pass that, in place of a profound interpretation of the eternally recurring problems, a historical—yea, even philological—balancing and questioning has entered into the educational arena: what this or that philosopher has or has not thought; whether this or that essay or dialogue is to be ascribed to him or not; or even whether this particular reading of a classical text is to be preferred to that. It is to neutral preoccupations with philosophy like these that our students in philosophical seminaries are stimulated; whence I have long accustomed myself to regard such science as a mere ramification of philology, and to value its representatives in proportion as they are good or bad philologists. So it has come about that *philosophy itself* is banished from the universities: wherewith our first question as to the value of our universities from the standpoint of culture is answered.[53]

One can imagine philologists feeling somewhat aggrieved by those words when Nietzsche uttered them on 23 March 1872. *Not* the public he was looking for in the main. Just as well he didn't publish a sequel (a sixth lecture was never delivered) as an *Unfashionable Observation* after all (*Afterphilologie*, so to speak). Recall in "We Philologists" that "ninety-nine philologists out of a hundred *should* not be philologists at all." Not content to insult his subordinates—although naturally some of those valiant "representatives" of the profession will be "good" philologists—he then threatens to put them out of a job. From our perspective—though Nietzsche perfectly envisions the horror of mass education—such tensions in the division of labour are simply part and parcel of the university, as a purely commercial institution, in its everyday operations.

Of course, it would be wrong simply to transplant Nietzsche's argument, which is equally to do with the *science of aesthetics*, into modern times as if nothing in the world had changed. Having said that, Nietzsche's speech displays all the philosophical blandness of a contemporary university vice chancellor. Now, admittedly, such impressions count for little, since reports to the academy belong to the realm of judgements, "feedback," and rules, not instances of philosophy.

That being said, however, if the task of philology is to stay quiet, not interfere, and keep the fires burning in the engine room of culture while the geniuses wait for inspiration to strike on the upper decks, then one can see why Nietzsche is so readily inclined to opt for philosophy over philology.[54] He can't rest indifferent to the destiny of free spirits. Can he have his cake and eat it?

The author of *The Birth of Tragedy*, despite dedicating the work to Richard Wagner, will refuse to follow the maestro's lead and address what were, in the latter's view, the *social* tensions responsible for holding genius back. As Wagner has it in his own art manifesto, written in 1848, and published a year later in somewhat different circumstances to 1871 and *its* aftermath:

> When the Brotherhood of Man has cast this care [subsistence labour] for ever from it, and, as the Greeks upon their slaves, has lain it on machines,—the artificial slaves of free creative man, whom he has served till now as the Fetish-votary serves the idol his own hands have made,—then will man's whole enfranchised energy proclaim itself as naught but pure artistic impulse.[55]

In the years since *Art and Revolution* was published—twenty-three, in fact, during which the Young Hegelian had plenty of time to come to his senses[56]—the situation had fundamentally changed. In 1848, Wagner was writing under the profound misapprehension that "artificial slaves" would *solve* the social question and, in so doing, solve the artistic question too. But in reality, they did the opposite. "It is questionable if all the mechanical inventions yet made have lightened the day's toil of any human being."[57] For Karl Marx, the purpose behind mechanical inventions is not to *relieve* workers of their burden; on the contrary, the *intensification* of labour is machinery's defining economic motivation.[58] What Wagner fails dismally to recognise, then, in *Art and Revolution*—whereas Nietzsche sees it perfectly well—is that *human* slaves exist *for the benefit of art*, which simply *could not* exist without them. This is why for Nietzsche, whose *Birth of Tragedy* is gestating as the "Louvre burns" and during the siege of Metz (his "Waiting for Godot" moment when nothing happens), the industrial "slaves" (read: communards) cannot be liberated from subsistence labour, lest they run riot. In *The Birth of Tragedy*, Schopenhauerian pessimism is the order of the day, on the social question at least, and one will parse the text in vain for a single reference to socially liberating technology.[59] Indeed, crucially, recall that the Dionysiac impulse in *The Birth of Tragedy* has nothing remotely political about it, any more than the Greek slaves—whose only (symbolic) respite from slavery came on festival days—had anything remotely political about them.

What does all this amount to, at least in Nietzsche's eyes? For the historical Nietzsche, the one who proudly dedicates his musical manifesto to Wagner, genius can rest easy, in principle at least. His book is the proof. Whereas those dutiful beasts of burden, the Basel philologists, might have rather more to worry about. And yet the burden of genius cuts both ways. Recall that Nietzsche will end his days as a scribbler of independent means, a self-publishing pamphleteer, and not at all the distinguished man of letters who stands before academies. The man of letters will become a scattered letter writer, a sceptical philologist, exposing forgeries in the texts as much as in his own life. In future, the algorithm will run just as slowly as it had in the academic address of 1872—delivered at Basel's city museum "without haste"[60]—while losing none of the precision (the pedantries?) of its techne. As he would affirm in the Preface to *Daybreak*:

> It is not for nothing that I have been a philologist, perhaps I am a philologist still, that is to say, a teacher of slow reading:—in the end I also write slowly. Nowadays it is not only my habit, it is also to my taste—a malicious taste, perhaps?—no longer to write anything which does not reduce to despair every sort of man who is "in a hurry." For philology is that venerable art which demands of its votaries one thing above all: to go aside, to take time, to become still, to become slow.[61]

Would it be possible to parse the Nietzsche archives with the aim of providing, on the literary evidence, some *model* of the real man? But then, even if it were, what would that prove about "Nietzsche"? Would it be as simple as prefixing to the ancient name of Mount Athos and its spiritually disturbed Hesychasts a plosive of some kind, whether a "B" or a "P," whether voiced or voiceless?[62] In the end, it turns out, once again, that the spasm of an equivocal, inexistent, *a-thetic* plosive returns, unevaluable, in even the most profound and superficial efforts of *philia* to articulate itself with either *Logos* or *Sophia*. The birth is never accomplished, the baby is never quite born, there is nothing stable but the volatile and crazy imputations of a *bereshit* behind the masks.

1 "– the will to power not a being, not a becoming, but a *pathos*, is the most elemental fact, and becoming, effecting, is only a result of this . . ." Friedrich Nietzsche, *Writings from the Late Notebooks*, ed. Rüdiger Bittner, trans. Kate Sturge (Cambridge University Press, 2003), 247. Indeed, from the beginning to the end of his work, Nietzsche identifies and analyses, with exquisite care, the genesis, ambitions, and varieties of the modifications of pathos: So we find the *Pathos der Richtertum*, *Pathos der Distanz*, *Pathos der Wahrheit* . . . Hence, as Alenka Zupančič writes, even Nietzsche's style expresses "the pathos of life. This is also the source of the comic component of Nietzsche's style—it arises not from a reflective distance toward life . . . but from life reflecting upon itself in an entirely immanent way." *The Shortest Shadow: Nietzsche's Philosophy of the Two* (MIT Press, 2003), 4.

2 Alain Badiou, "Who is Nietzsche?," *Pli* 11 (2001): 2.

3 Friedrich Nietzsche, "Attempt at a Self-Criticism," in *The Birth of Tragedy*, trans. Douglas Smith (Oxford University Press, 2000), 12–13.

4 "The University of Life," whether being used facetiously or not, is a term that somewhat captures this supposedly natural hierarchy. Ironically, or perhaps not, universities of life *sciences* are nowadays quite widespread. The so-called "School of Life" (not a teaching institution) was founded in 2008 by Alain de Botton and other media savvy entrepreneurs. Here we encounter the self-help guru dispensing doses of wisdom in motivational manuals and podcasts.

5 John Tyndall, *Fragments of Science: A Series of Detached Essays, Addresses, and Reviews*, vol. 2 (Longmans, Green and Co., 1879), 93.

6 See Kostas Axelos, *The Game of the World*, trans. Justin Clemens and Hellmut Monz (Edinburgh University Press, 2023), *passim*.

7 Here, the testimony of his Inaugural Professorial Address at Basel is imperative: "Philology at every period from its origin onwards was at the same time pedagogical." Friedreich Nietzsche, *Homer and Classical Philology*, in *The Complete Works of Friedrich Nietzsche*, vol. 3, ed. Oscar Levy, trans. J. M. Kennedy (Edinburgh and T. N. Foulis, 1910), para 1, https://www.gutenberg.org/cache/epub/18188/pg18188-images.html.

8 Friedrich Nietzsche, *Unfashionable Observations*, trans. Richard T. Gray (Stanford University Press, 1995), 229–30.

9 Nietzsche, *Unfashionable Observations*, 255.

10 Friedrich Nietzsche, *On the Future of Our Educational Institutions*, trans. J. M. Kennedy (T. N. Foulis, 1910), 126–7.

11 "Supposing one were to imagine a philosopher as a great educator, powerful enough to stand on his lonely heights and pull long chains of generations up to him: Then one would also have to grant him the uncanny prerogatives of the great educator. An educator never says what he himself is thinking, but always only what he thinks about a thing in relation to its use to the one he is educating. He must not be detected in this dissemblance; it is part of his mastery that we believe in his honesty." Friedrich Nietzsche, *Unpublished Fragments (Spring 1885–Spring 1886)*, ed. Duncan Large and Alan D. Schrift, trans. Adrian Del Caro,

The Complete Works of Friedrich Nietzsche, volume 16 (Stanford University Press, 2020), 36–37.

12 Laurence Lampert, *Nietzsche and Modern Times: A Study of Bacon, Descartes, and Nietzsche* (Yale University Press, 1993), 7.

13 Elie During, "Deleuze and Nietzsche: On Frivolous Propositions and Related Matters," *Pli* 11 (2001): 71. During's point here is that philological speculation is neither frivolous nor false—if it is not necessarily true, it is in the service of the reconstruction of lost, damaged, hidden constructions.

14 See Friedrich Nietzsche, *The Dionysian Vision of the World*, trans. Ira J. Allen (University of Minnesota Press, 2013).

15 Hannah Arendt, *The Human Condition* (University of Chicago Press, 1958), 248.

16 Jean-Claude Milner, Ann Banfield, and Daniel Heller-Roazen, "Interview with Jean-Claude Milner," *S: Journal of the Circle for Lacanian Ideology Critique* 3 (2010): 4.

17 Milner, 5.

18 Werner Hamacher and Catharine Diehl, "95 Theses on Philology," *Diacritics* 39, no. 1 (2009): 40–41.

19 "Nietzsche began as an admirer of Luther and the German Reformation. The age of Luther ranked as high in his early opinion as the age of Goethe and Beethoven. From *Menschliches, Allzumenschliches* on, this favorable attitude towards Luther underwent a strong transformation. In the five years from 1878 to 1883, Nietzsche's second creative period, Luther emerged as a highly questionable figure, even as a most regrettable event in the history of German and European thought and civilization. But all these severe pronouncements on Luther were only a prelude to the scathing denunciations to come in Nietzsche's post-Zarathustra writings." Heinz Bluhm, "Nietzsche's final view of Luther and the Reformation," *PMLA*, vol. 71, no. 1 (1956), 75.

20 See James I. Porter, "'Don't Quote Me on That!': Wilamowitz Contra Nietzsche in 1872 and 1873" in *Journal of Nietzsche Studies* 42, no. 1 (2011): 73–99.

21 "For though the sleeping body then lies as if it were dead, yet the soul is alive and strong." Erwin Rohde, *Psyche. The Cult of Souls and Belief in Immortality among the Greeks*, trans. W. B. Hillis (Kegan Paul, Trench, Trubner & Co., 1925), 44. Rohde's citation from Cicero's *De Divinatione* continues: "*Quod multo magis faciet post mortem cum omnino corpore excesserit*"/ "and will be much more so after death when it is wholly free of the body." *De Senectute De Amicitia De Divinatione*, trans. William Armistead Falconer (Harvard University Press, 1923), i, 63.

22 See Porter, "Don't Quote Me on That!," 86.

23 Friedrich Nietzsche, "Why I Write Such Good Books," in *Ecce Homo*, trans. Duncan Large (Oxford University Press), 37. One could cite countless passages in the same vein.

24 Friedrich Nietzsche, "We Philologists," in *The Complete Works of Friedrich Nietzsche Volume 8*, eds. Oscar Levy and trans. J. M. Kennedy (T. N. Foulis, 1911), 110.

25 Nietzsche, "We Philologists," 110.

26 Nietzsche, 113.
27 Friedrich Nietzsche, *Selected Letters of Friedrich Nietzsche*, ed. and trans. Christopher Middleton (Hackett, 1996), 96.
28 Porter, "Don't Quote Me on That!," 98n.
29 Nietzsche, *Selected Letters of Friedrich Nietzsche*, 97.
30 Christopher Middleton notes: "The archaeological evidence adduced by Pickard-Cambridge (*Dithyramb: Tragedy and Comedy*, Cambridge University Press, 1927, 174) suggests that N was forcing this point: On sixth-century Greek pottery the satyrs are equine, not capriform—not goat figures at all, but horse demons, wearing horse tails. Pickard-Cambridge maintains that the capriform satyr was a relatively late (fifth-century) invention." *Selected Letters of Friedrich Nietzsche,* 97n.
31 James I. Porter, *Nietzsche and the Philology of the Future* (Stanford University Press, 2000).
32 Porter, *Nietzsche and the Philology of the Future,* 33.
33 Porter, 36; Nietzsche, *Selected Letters of Friedrich Nietzsche*, 102.
34 Need we spell it out? How could Nietzsche ever resent or renounce being reduced to a mere footnote!
35 See Nietzsche's letter to Rohde of October 25, 1872 in *Selected Letters of Friedrich Nietzsche*, 103–105.
36 Friedrich Nietzsche, *Homer and Classical Philology*, para 20, https://www.gutenberg.org/cache/epub/18188/pg18188-images.html.
37 Nietzsche, *Homer and Classical Philology*, para 22.
38 Porter, *Nietzsche and the Philology of the Future,* 37–40.
39 As far as theories of *algorithmic* randomness are concerned, however—note algorithmic, not *stochastic* randomness—let us note that Gregory Chaitin *defines* such randomness as an incomputable data string requiring as many symbols to *describe* as the string itself consists of. See G. J. Chaitin, "Algorithmic Information Theory," in *IBM Journal of Research and Development*, no. 4 (1977): 350–59.
40 Nietzsche, "Why I Write Such Good Books," 48.
41 Porter, *Nietzsche and the Philology of the Future,* 36.
42 Porter, 37.
43 The key word here is "ultimately." Chaitin, "Algorithmic Information Theory," 355: "At the high-order end of the complexity scale for infinite strings are the random strings, and the recursive strings are at the low order end." Chaitin further remarks that "a formal axiomatic theory is valuable for the same reason as a scientific theory; in both cases information is being compressed, and one is also concerned with the tradeoff between the degree of compression and the length of proofs of interesting theorems or the time required to compute predictions," 357. We wonder how this "tradeoff" might work in Nietzschean philology between "interesting theorems" and the necessary labour-time of their proofs.
44 Porter, *Nietzsche and the Philology of the Future,* 37. This is a philologically *un*-sceptical statement by Porter. Let us add in the same breath: *As a grammatical expression*. The *sceptical* philological question might be, instead, to decide whether "Democritus" is in fact distinguishable from "Nietzsche's conception of him,"

or whether there is *provably* at least one conception that isn't a paradox.

45 Christopher Middleton, "Preface," in *Selected Letters of Friedrich Nietzsche*, ix.

46 Domenico Losurdo, *Nietzsche, The Aristocratic Rebel. Intellectual Biography and Critical Balance Sheet*, trans. Gregor Benton (Haymarket Books, 2021).

47 Nietzsche, *On the Future of Our Educational Institutions*, 128.

48 Immanuel Kant, *Critique of the Power of Judgment*, eds. and trans. Paul Guyer and Eric Matthews (Cambridge University Press, 2013), 187.

49 On reflection, the vocation of the genius is not so very different from that of the non-genius. Consider the university student who, during Jacques Lacan's so-called impromptu talk at Vincennes University on 3 December 1969, admitted to not knowing what "aphasic" meant, which they then justified by saying: "I am not at the university twenty-four hours a day." Clearly, the student has understood Kant's aesthetic precepts that, quite irrespective of how much they study, it won't make them a genius. The insight could be generalised, to the extent that university students, in our experience, will very often have absolutely no idea what they are learning, or what they are supposed to be doing in university; until, perhaps, they receive their "grade"; at which point they invariably still won't, since grades, somewhat like genius, will most often have no intelligible relation to the study which they don't understand. See Jacques Lacan, *The Seminar of Jacques Lacan Book XVII*, trans. R. Grigg (Norton, 2007), 206.

50 Kant, *Critique of the Power of Judgment*, 186.

51 Kant, 187.

52 Nietzsche, *On the Future of our Educational Institutions*, 115

53 Nietzsche, 130.

54 For Nietzsche, genius must transcend mass culture in order to achieve the "hierarchy of spirits; yea, a kind of pre-established harmony." His example is the "comical spectacle" of a German orchestra in rehearsal: "But set a genius—a real genius—in the midst of this crowd; and you instantly perceive something almost incredible. It is as if this genius, in his lightning transmigration, had entered into these mechanical bodies, and as if only one demoniacal eye gleamed forth out of them all . . . When you again observe the orchestra, now loftily storming, now fervently wailing, when you notice the quick tightening of every muscle and the rhythmical necessity of every gesture, then you too will feel what a pre-established harmony there is between leader and followers": Nietzsche, *On the Future of our Educational Institutions*, 143.

55 Richard Wagner, *Art and Revolution*, trans. William Ashton Ellis (Blackmask Online, 2002), np.

56 Along with Carl August Röckel and Mikhail Bakunin, Wagner was the main architect of the Dresden Uprising of May 1849. See Ernest Newman, *The Life of Richard Wagner, Volume 2: 1848–1860* (Alfred A. Knopf, 1937).

57 J. S. Mill, *Principles of Political Economy* (Batoche Books, 2001), 883. Marx quotes this dictum at the incipit to "Chapter 15: Machinery and Large-Scale Industry," in *Capital. A Critique of Political Economy, Volume One*, trans. Ben Fowkes (Penguin, 1990), 492.

58 Marx, *Capital*, 533–42.

59 In *The Aristocratic Rebel*, Domenico Losurdo observes that the Dionysian "superior community" imagined by Nietzsche in *The Birth of Tragedy* is grounded in a sociopolitical distinction between "the Apolline sphere" of art, beauty, and civilization, and the "Dionysiac sphere" which, despite bearing the suffering of civilization, "was not a determined social class" (63). Babette Babich indicates Nietzsche's umbrella term *Wissenschaft* in *Birth of Tragedy* to combine "logic and rationality as well as both the functioning of machines allegorically and literally, including the mechanized way of life of modernity." Babich, "Nietzsche's Philology and Nietzsche's Science: On the 'Problem of Science' and 'fröhliche Wissenschaft,'" in Pascale Hummel, ed., *Metaphilology: Histories and Languages of Philology* (Philologicum, 2009), 183. In the text itself, there is Nietzsche's famous allusion to the Alexandrian form that "replaces metaphysical consolation with a worldly consonance, even with its own *deus ex machina*—namely the god of machines and melting-pots, that is, the powers of the natural spirits which are known and used in the service of higher egoism." *The Birth of Tragedy*, 96.

60 Nietzsche, *On the Future of our Educational Institutions*, 4.

61 Nietzsche, *Daybreak: Thoughts on the Prejudices of Morality*, eds. Maudemarie Clark and Brian Leiter, trans. R. J. Hollingdale (Cambridge University Press, 1997), 5.

62 See Nietzsche, *On the Genealogy of Morality*, ed. Keith Ansell-Pearson, trans. Carol Diethe (Cambridge University Press, 2006), 97.

Nietzsche's *The Birth of Tragedy*: A Philosophy of Duality, Conflict, and Relationality

Vanessa Lemm

Nietzsche's *The Birth of Tragedy*

This chapter offers a reading of the opening sentence of Nietzsche's *The Birth of Tragedy*:

> We shall have gained much for the science of aesthetics when we have come to realize, not just through logical insight but also with the certainty of something directly apprehended (*unmittelbaren Sicherheit der Anschauung*), that the continuous development (*Fortentwicklung*) of art is bound up with the duality (*Duplicitaet*) of the *Apollonian* and the *Dionysian* in much the same way as reproduction (Generation) depends on the duality (*Zweiheit*) of the sexes in a state of perpetual conflict (*Kampf*) interrupted only occasionally by periods of reconciliation.[1]

> *Wir werden viel für die aesthetische Wissenschaft gewonnen haben, wenn wir nicht nur zur logischen Einsicht, sondern zur unmittelbaren Sicherheit der Anschauung gekommen sind, dass die Fortentwickelung der Kunst an die Duplicität des Apollinischen und des Dionysischen gebunden ist: in ähnlicher Weise, wie die Generation von der Zweiheit der Geschlechter, bei fortwährendem Kampfe und nur periodisch eintretender Versöhnung, abhängt.*[2]

I shall argue that this sentence sets the tone for the entire book and, beyond *The Birth of Tragedy*, informs the future direction of Nietzsche's philosophy. I am tempted to say that the opening sentence offers a summary right at the start, with the remainder of the book reflecting perhaps nothing but an exegesis of its opening statement. My reading is guided by this book's title, interrogating the relationship between tragedy, art, and philosophy. More specifically, I will pursue the question of philosophy and its relationship to the discovery of Apollonian and Dionysian life forces, whose continuous struggle is bound up with the generation of life and the enhancement of art. My approach to this question is philosophical and not aesthetic, and I will therefore not discuss the relationship between philosophy and aesthetics. Instead, this chapter is guided by an analysis of three conceptual clusters, namely: first, "*Duplicitaet*" (duality) and "*Zweiheit der Geschlechter*" (sexual difference);

second, "*Zweiheit*" (duality) and *Zwiespalt* (discord); and third, "*Kampf*" (struggle) and "*Versöhnung*" (reconciliation).

From the outset, Nietzsche's philosophy and way of philosophising is inseparably bound up with the notion of Zweiheit. Nietzsche enters the stage of the philological, aesthetic, and philosophical debates of his time as a thinker of the "two" and remains faithful to this opening gesture of doubling throughout his philosophical life all the way to *Ecce Homo*.[3] In *Ecce Homo*, commenting on his early work, he notes that philosophy, like all public matters, is unthinkable outside of an arena of competition. This may explain why he wanted to follow Stendhal's advice "to make one's entry into society with a *duel*."[4] I read *The Birth of Tragedy*'s opening sentence as just such an entry.

I argue that Nietzsche is a thinker of relationality. In the reception of *The Birth of Tragedy*, Nietzsche's philosophy has often been falsely associated with a thinking of identity. Adrian Del Caro, for example, discards the work as a "romantic celebration of metaphysics" whose treatment of the Dionysian was "still very much under the influence of Richard Wagner and that man's anti-Semitic views."[5] According to Del Caro, it is only Nietzsche's later treatment of the Dionysian, post *Zarathustra*, that becomes "associated with new philosophizing."[6] By contrast, I seek to show that the book does not reflect a thinking of identity. Rather, it sets the path for the development of a philosophy of duality and perpetual conflict. Furthermore, I want to challenge those readings of *The Birth of Tragedy* that are, in my view, too rigid in their identification of Apollo and Dionysus as two separate and distinct figures, philosophical principles, or concepts. For example, John Sallis distinguishes Apollo and Dionysus as figures and "figural disclosures" of individuation (Apollo) and doubling (Dionysus), and Richard Schacht identifies Apollo with Nietzsche's notion of the overhuman and Dionysus with his notion of will to power.[7] These gestures of "identification" thereby lose sight of what I take to be the key finding of *The Birth of Tragedy*, namely, that it is the ambiguous, doubling, and conflicting nature of the *relationship* between Apollo and Dionysus itself that motivates the generation of art and life.

In the first part, "Duplicitaet and the Duality of the Sexes (Zweiheit der Geschlechter)," I trace the concept of Duplicitaet back to Kant and biological discourses on sexual reproduction. The different meaning of Duplicitaet and Zweiheit is lost in the English translation. Ronald Speirs, for example, translates Duplicitaet as "duality" and Zweiheit as "two."[8] Since the English translation does not fully capture the multifaceted meanings of these terms, I will refer to the German text. Duplicitaet is a technical term that refers to the law of polarity according to which sexual difference is the basis of the generation of life. In the first part, I argue that Nietzsche's thinking about the relationship between Apollo and Dionysus and the creation of the Greek Attic tragedy is influenced by these new discourses in biology to the extent that he conceives the generation of art through the generation of life in nature. The key point I wish to make is that Nietzsche's thinking about the relationship between art and nature seeks to overcome what today we refer to as the nature–culture divide.[9]

In the second part, "Zweiheit and Zwiespalt: Philosophy in the Tragic Age of the Greeks," I consider the notions of Zweiheit and Zwiespalt against the background of Nietzsche's interpretation of the Pre-Socratics, to show that the Zweiheit of Dionysus and Apollo is not an opposition between two stable and fixed entities, and, furthermore, that it does not dissolve into a higher unity, whether that of being as in Anaximander or that of thought as in Parmenides. Instead, the Zweiheit of Dionysus and Apollo is affirmed within the eternal movement of becoming, that is, within the continuous movement of struggle and conflict through which both the Dionysian and the Apollonian life forces continue to define and redefine themselves in the generation of life and the work of art. According to my reading, Zweiheit does not refer to a splitting of Apollo and Dionysus into two separate entities. Rather, Zweiheit means Zwiespalt, revealing an ambiguity, mix-up, and entanglement of two that cannot be dissolved into one. Nietzsche's conception of Zweiheit signals the priority of relation over identity, intuition over logical insight, plurality over unity.

In the third and concluding part, "Kampf (Struggle) and Versöhnung (Reconciliation)," I consider Nietzsche's conception of "*Einheit*" (unity) as it is reflected in his thoughts on personal and interpersonal, social, and political relationships. I argue that Nietzsche's pairing of Apollo and Dionysus is creative only when their crossing and unity maintain the productive tension between Zweiheit and Zwiespalt, struggle and reconciliation. When the Dionysian and the Apollonian are in balance, the Duplicitaet between Dionysus and Apollo manifests itself as a creating together. Nietzsche sees such a fruitful coming together of Dionysus and Apollo reflected in Greek tragedy. This creative balance between Dionysus and Apollo, struggle and reconciliation, turns under the rule of Socratism and his agent Euripides into the domination of one life force by another, resulting in the end of the Attic tragedy and the decline of Greek culture.

I.
Duplicitaet and the Duality of the Sexes (Zweiheit der Geschlechter)

In his published writings, Nietzsche will use the term Duplicitaet only once in the opening sentence of *The Birth of Tragedy* and in two notes leading up to the publication of the 1872 edition.[10] As has been documented by Barbara Riebnitz in her commentary to the work, Nietzsche takes the term Duplicitaet from Kant's *Anthropology*, where it refers to an emerging biological discourse on the reproduction of life.[11] The term Duplicitaet is a reference to this biological law of polarity (*Gesetz der Polarität*), which underpins the idea that everything in nature emerges from Zweiheit. Reibnitz argues that Kant's reflections on the law of polarity have influenced philosophers of nature with a Romantic orientation, such as F. W. J. Schelling and J. W. Görres, who conceive of Duplicitaet as a general law according to which the development of nature follows a general conflict between negative and positive principles, and maintain that, without their opposing forces, living movement would not be possible.[12] But Romantic philosophies of nature were certainly not the only influence on Nietzsche's early thinking about nature. According to Carlotta Santini, the material Nietzsche collected for an unfinished dissertation titled "On the Concept of the Organic since Kant" draws on the metaphor of the living organism to explain the internal processes of growth and decline that preside over the development of historical and cultural phenomena, reflecting the "strong attraction" post-Kantian biological discourses must have exerted on the young philosopher.[13] In the context of these biological discourses, Duplicitaet is considered a "technical term," which would explain why Nietzsche will not use it after *The Birth of Tragedy*.

Leaving the question of influence aside for a moment, it seems noteworthy that Nietzsche establishes, right at the beginning of his book, a fundamental relationship between nature and art. Just as the generation of life is underpinned by the "law of polarity," so too the generation of art is dependent on the Duplicitaet of Apollonian and Dionysian life forces. The generation of life and art follow the same principle, which may explain why Nietzsche will adopt the perspective of life as the focal viewpoint of his philosophical analysis. As he writes in the preface from 1886, the task of his book was and has remained the same, namely, "to look at science through the prism of the artist, but also to look at art through the prism of life."[14] For Wolfgang Riedel, the crossing of the new biological discourses of the eighteenth and nineteenth centuries within philosophy generates a paradigm shift from philosophies of nature (*Naturphilosophie*) to philosophies of life (*Lebensphilosophie*).[15] *The Birth of Tragedy* marks a key turning point in this new approach to philosophy.

According to Riedel, the sexualisation of nature is a phenomenon that has marked the development of literary anthropology since 1900, conceiving human nature through new discourses of drives, passions, and animality. I would suggest that this "trend" is already reflected in Nietzsche's opening statement of *The Birth of Tragedy*, which centrally positions sexual difference and the struggle between the sexes in his thesis on the Duplicitaet between the Apollonian and the Dionysian drives in their relation to the future generation of life and art.[16] At the centre of these new discourses stand the body and sexuality. This paradigm shift towards the body and its sexuality no doubt reflects the entry of biological science as the new episteme of the nineteenth century, along with the discovery of reproduction and sexuality. It leads to a new understanding of nature as living nature, that is as a living being with reproduction as the key feature of life.[17] In this paradigm, the same mechanism of reproduction (sexuality) is shared by all forms of life and can be traced all the way to the life of individual cells. For Riedel, the life sciences of Nietzsche's time confirm that nature is becoming, that life is a continuous flow and exchange of cells, and that self-production is nothing but a continuous death where death becomes just an instance of life and life another instance of death. Life is both creation and destruction, sensuality and cruelty, Eros and Thanatos.[18] What stands in the foreground is no longer simply the life of the individual and its striving for self-preservation. Rather, the latter needs to be understood as an instance of the life of the species and its drive for reproduction.

According to Riedel, this new anthropology finds one of its first iterations in Schopenhauer's philosophy of the will and the view that "the human being is concretely sex drive (*Geschlechtstrieb*) . . . The sex drive is the fullest expression of the will to life."[19] In the notion of the will, Schopenhauer attempts to grasp the strangeness and otherness of nature within the human intellect, and as something that is active and creative in all organic processes, which is also reflected in Nietzsche's philosophical anthropology.[20] However, what is new with Nietzsche and what distinguishes his treatment of sexuality from that of Schopenhauer is the way in which he takes up the socialisation of sexuality in the nineteenth century in his thinking about sexual difference. For Nietzsche, the struggle between the sexes is perhaps in reality the urtext of Greek tragedies.

Against this background, Nietzsche's reference to the term Duplicitaet cannot exclusively be associated with Romantic natural philosophy, as Reibnitz seems to suggest. Rather, as Riedel argues, we need to take into consideration both the biological discourses of the nineteenth century and post-Kantian natural philosophy to arrive at a new conception of life and of a philosophy of life that is taking shape in *The Birth of Tragedy*.[21] In contrast to the biological discourses of his time, for Nietzsche, the natural forces and drives of life remain withdrawn from "logical insight" and only come to be "apprehended directly through intuition (Anschauung)."[22] Intuition reveals that nature is "terrible" (*schrecklich*), governed by a strife and struggle that holds the pairings of Apollo and Dionysus, male and female, human and animal, in continuous tension, engaged in enmity and Zwiespalt that cannot be translated into a "universal law" of nature, as Romantic philosophies of nature suggest.

From Nietzsche's vantage point, the Dionysian and the Apollonian are forces of nature, or, in other words, nature itself is the artist: "the Apollonian and its opposite, the Dionysian, as artistic powers which erupt from nature itself, without the mediation of any human artist, and in which nature's artistic drives attain their first, immediate satisfaction."[23] Nietzsche's conception of giving artistic form to life assumes that nature is itself artistic. In a note from the same period, he writes: "What is creative (*schafft*) there [in nature], what creates artistically (*künstlerisch schafft*), is active (*wirkt*) in the artist."[24] As such, Nietzsche's conception of art and the "science of aesthetics" that *The Birth of Tragedy* seeks to advance is based on an overcoming of the separation between art and nature. The work reflects an attempt to think together Dionysus and Apollo in view of bridging the divide between nature and art, philosophy and aesthetics, life and culture. In this context, it is important to note, as Claus Zittel points out, that the overall metaphysical structure of *The Birth of Tragedy* is based on further divisions, polarities, and splitting. In addition to the duality between Dionysus and Apollo in *The Birth of Tragedy*, Nietzsche insists that the *Ur-Grund* or *Ur-Eine* is always already torn and split within itself, suffering from itself, and therefore creative and in need of appearance for its salvation. As such, the *Ur-Grund* is always already double and therefore a creative primal artist for whom the individual artist is only a means.[25]

Nature is per se creative, and there is no dichotomy, separation, or disconnection between nature and art.[26]

According to Sallis, the Apollinian and Dionysian "are states of nature by which nature will in a sense always have anticipated art, states of nature in which there is already, in the direction of art, a certain monstrous break with nature, complicating the classical opposition between nature and art even before the advent of the human artist."[27] Sallis captures the relationship between art and nature, or nature and itself, through the figure of the "monstrous break," which resonates with the monstrous opposition (*ungeheure Gegensatz*) between Apollo and Dionysus to which Nietzsche refers in the opening passage to introduce the two key figures of his book. In contrast to Sallis, I suggest that the monstrous opposition between Apollo and Dionysus, art and nature, does not stand for a break from nature or within nature. Rather, the Duplicitaet of Apollo and Dionysus reveals a continuity with and within nature to the extent that Apollo and Dionysus, art and nature, present an impenetrable (and hence uncanny) mix and entanglement that lies beyond the reach of "logical insight." The Duplicitaet of Apollo and Dionysus is impenetrable and ultimately inconceivable, which is why it requires "immediate intuition," rather than "logical insight," to capture and conceive their crossing in the "profound mysteries" (*tiefsinnige Geheimlehre*) of the Greeks' views on art.

In a recent article, Claus Zittel makes the ironic observation that while half of the world is celebrating and commemorating the 150th anniversary of *The Birth of Tragedy*, very few people are actually familiar with the 1872 edition of the book.[28] Apart from rectifying an omission in the history of a (mis)reception of Nietzsche's work, the key argument put forward by Zittel is that the first edition of 1872 is much more "nihilistic, poetic, and powerful" because it exhibits the strong influence of Hebbel's tragic worldview. In the first edition, Greek art stood in the foreground, and the dualism between Apollo and Dionysus was understood as a mere reflection of aesthetic stylistic principles found in the Attic tragedy. This worldview is obscured in the second edition, written under the influence of Wagner, where the opposition between Apollo and Dionysus is now conceived as a fundamental antagonism between forces of nature. In the second edition, Nietzsche's position becomes more distinctly philosophical, and *the birth of tragedy* is said to have been conceived through "a metaphysical miracle of the Hellenic 'Will.'"[29] Interestingly, the first sentence of *The Birth of Tragedy* remains unchanged across the various editions of the book. I take this as an indicator that, despite a shift from the first to the second edition towards philosophy and away from aesthetics, the predominance of the Dionysian over the Apollonian, intuition over logical insight, remains constant for Nietzsche.

This would explain why, for Nietzsche, the generation of both life and art is inherently dependent on our ability to reconnect with what he refers to as the "mythical," a term which he also uses as another name for the Dionysian. Only through the mythical can we overcome the denial of the creativity of nature and recover the artistic forces of nature that inform the generation of both life and art. In other words, we need to first acknowledge the key role of relationality in Nietzsche's conception of art and nature before we can understand the figure of disruption which, according to Sallis, marks the emergence of culture within nature. Adopting the terminology of Roberto Esposito, we could say that Nietzsche's thinking about art and nature is in the first instance "communitary" and reflects a relationship "without subject" between Apollo and Dionysus that both precedes and disrupts the "immunitary" separation between nature and culture.[30] The immunitary function of art, by contrast, is reflected in Nietzsche's description of the dissimulating function of art as it produces a "metaphysical supplement of the reality of nature, placed beside it for its overcoming."[31]

Although Nietzsche praises the healing force of the Apollonian dream as it dissimulates and transfigures the unbearable vision of the world as an abyss, ultimately what reconciles humanity with life, nature, and one another is the "magic of the Dionysian": "Not only is the bond between human beings renewed by the magic of the Dionysian, but nature, alienated, inimical, or subjugated, celebrated once more her festival of reconciliation with her lost son, humankind."[32] What is "magic" about the Dionysian is that it binds, touches, and connects, which is why it must be understood as a relational force. Under the impact of Dionysian magic, the human being affirms and celebrates its naturalness and connection with the natural world as a source of life and culture. Only when surrounded by the Dionysian myth can the Apollonian dream preserve itself and be given a direction.[33] The Dionysian leads the Apollonian just as nature leads the human artist towards the generation of life and art.

In *The Birth of Tragedy*, Nietzsche returns to the image of the life of plants and roots to signal our disconnection from an archaic and mythical conception of nature. For him, the future of life and art depends on our capacity to re-root ourselves in the mythical and natural: "But how suddenly the wilderness of our tired culture, which we have just painted in such gloomy colours, can be transformed, when it is touched by the Dionysian magic."[34] Through the Dionysian, Nietzsche puts forward a conception of human nature as an instance of interdependent and interrelated life that deeply defines who we are and what our purpose is in and through our relationship to other forms of life. The opening sentence articulates this relationship through sexual difference, and it is perhaps here that we find a point of difference between Kant's and Nietzsche's reflections on Duplicitaet and the "law of polarity."

While he was working on a first draft of *The Birth of Tragedy*, Nietzsche remarked: "Kant once said that the natural arrangement (*Natureinrichtung*) by which all reproduction is linked up with the duality of the sexes (*Duplicität des Geschlechts*), struck him as astonishing and as an abyss of thought for human reason."[35] In a draft from April 1871, he translates this note into his reflections on tragedy:

> The fact that nature linked the origin of tragedy to those two fundamental drives, the Apollonian and the Dionysian, may be regarded as an abyss of reason just as much as the device by which in nature propagation is linked up with the duality of the sexes: what struck the great Kant as astonishing.

> The common secret is namely how something new can arise from two mutually hostile principles, in which those conflicting (*zwiespältigen*) drives appear as a unity: in which sense propagation may count just as much as the tragic work of art as a guarantee of the rebirth of Dionysus, as a ray of hope on the eternally mourning face of Demeter.[36]

Whereas Kant's reflection on the duality of the sexes found in nature confronts human reason with the incomprehensible and abyssal aspects of procreation, generation, and reproduction, Nietzsche draws our attention to the secret of creation and creativity reflected in the miraculous coming together of "two mutually hostile principles," two "conflicting (zwiespältigen) drives" into "unity," here the tragic work of art. Whereas Kant stops at the contemplation of the abyss, the experience of the sublime, Nietzsche affirms the abyssal character of life as the birthplace of creativity.

As the title of *The Birth of Tragedy* suggests, Nietzsche proposes a new idea of birth that challenges and redefines the semantic fields of "pregnancy," "sexuality," and "creation" that have hitherto been associated with the Socratic "method" in philosophy. According to David Wellbery, birth is the abyss of thought, and as such it is the origin of tragedy: "Tragedy itself is born of birth as the rationally incomprehensible abyss. This is the guiding insight of Nietzsche's *Birth of Tragedy*."[37] What distinguishes Nietzsche's conception of birth from that of Socrates, who for Plato is the "midwife" of virtue and knowledge,[38] is that it reflects an experience of transgression that rests on an affirmation of birth as the site of "an experience of non-identity, which is rooted in the human being's being born."[39] For Wellbery, *The Birth of Tragedy* is not merely a text about aesthetics reflecting an aesthetic conception of life; rather, it offers an "ontology of birth" that seeks to overcome the Socratic-theoretical worldview by problematising the fact of "the radical contingency of living on."[40] From Wellbery's perspective, the aesthetic justification of life derives from the idea that every human being becomes like Demeter, whose only hope is to give birth again to Dionysus—or, in other words, the continuous reaffirmation of birth as the site of non-identity, difference, and doubling.[41] This brings me back to the main argument of this chapter, namely showing that Nietzsche is a thinker of the two, of difference and plurality.

II.
Zweiheit und Zwiespalt: Philosophy in the Tragic Age of the Greeks

In the opening passage of *The Birth of Tragedy*, Nietzsche describes the duality of Apollo and Dionysus as a "monstrous opposition" (*ungeheuren Gegensatz*) and "open conflict" (*offnen Zwiespalt*).[42] Their relationship functions as a prototype of the many other "doubles" and "doublings" that we find throughout his work: culture–nature, human–animal, man–woman, and slave–noble, to name just a few. These pairings reflect movements of doubling that go back to Nietzsche's discovery of the Dionysian, its relationship to the Apollonian, and the emergence of Greek tragedy, which is one reason why the work continues to be such an important reference point for contemporary aesthetics and philosophy. In the reception of Nietzsche's philosophy, as mentioned above, *The Birth of Tragedy* is at times dismissed due to its author's over-identification with Wagner's aesthetic and political views, reinforcing the need to continue to demonstrate that the work does not reflect a thinking of identity.

So far, we have considered the relevance of Kant's reflection on Duplicitaet and the biological discourses on sexual difference for Nietzsche's thinking about the conflictual tension between Apollonian and Dionysian life forces at the basis of natural generation and artistic creation. However, a different context to Nietzsche's use of the concept Zweiheit in *The Birth of Tragedy* is provided by his early text on philosophy in the tragic age of the Greeks.[43] Nietzsche employs the term Zweiheit in his discussion of Anaximander and Heraclitus. Whereas for the former there exist two worlds, a physical world and a metaphysical world, the latter rejects this conception of Zweiheit. As Nietzsche summarises, "firstly, he denied the duality (Zweiheit) of two quite diverse worlds, into the assumption of which Anaximander had been pushed; he no longer distinguished a physical world from a metaphysical, a realm of definite qualities from a realm of indefinable indefiniteness."[44]

Heraclitus denies Anaximander's denial of the world of becoming. Henceforth, Heraclitus' affirmation that everything is becoming is underpinned by "two coherent negations."[45] First, the denial of "two quite diverse worlds," and second, the denial of Being altogether: "Now after this first step, he could neither be kept back any longer from a still greater audacity of denying: He denied Being altogether."[46] This discussion is important in clarifying Nietzsche's own conception of the abyss of nature (the splitting and doubling of the *Ur-Grund*) in *The Birth of Tragedy*, which is often in the literature associated with a "rest" of metaphysics, with a Kantian idea of the thing in itself.[47]

Zweiheit and the associated movement of negation thus have a double connotation: with Heraclitus, Nietzsche rejects a conception of Zweiheit as a stable and fixed opposition of terms, such as the two worlds in Anaximander. However, again with Heraclitus, Nietzsche also affirms a different conception of Zweiheit that alludes to plurality and multiplicity. Here, Zweiheit as plurality is affirmed within Heraclitus' conception of becoming as opposed to Anaximander's conception of Being:

> For this one world which was left to him,—shielded all round by eternal, unwritten laws, flowing up and down in the brazen beat of rhythm,—shows nowhere persistence, indestructibility, a bulwark in the stream. Louder than Anaximander, Heraclitus exclaimed: "I see nothing but Becoming . . . You need names for things, just as if they had a rigid permanence, but the very river in which you bathe a second time is no longer the same one which you entered before."[48]

This double movement also underpins Nietzsche's position towards Parmenides. Whereas Heraclitus's idea of becoming includes and affirms Zweiheit as plurality and multiplicity,

Parmenides seeks to overcome Zweiheit as both plurality (Heraclitus) and opposition (Anaximander) in the oneness of thought and Being:

> Thinking and that one increate perfect ball of the Existent were now no longer to be conceived as two different kinds of Being, since there was not permitted a duality (Zweiheit) of Being. Thus, the over-risky flash of fancy had become necessary to declare Thinking and Being identical. No form of perceptibility, no symbol, no simile could possibly be of any help here; the fancy was wholly inconceivable, but it was necessary, yea in the lack of every possibility of illustration it celebrated the highest triumph over the world and the claims of the senses.[49]

A consideration of Nietzsche's interpretation of the Pre-Socratics shows that the Zweiheit of Dionysus and Apollo is not an opposition between two stable and fixed entities. Furthermore, the Zweiheit of Dionysus and Apollo does not dissolve into a higher unity, whether that of being, as in Anaximander, or that of thought, as in Parmenides. Instead, the Zweiheit of Dionysus and Apollo is affirmed within the eternal movement of becoming, that is, the continuous movement of struggle and conflict through which both the Dionysian and the Apollonian life forces continue to define and redefine themselves in the generation of the work of art.

In Sallis, the Apollonian and Dionysian are presented as entities or figures—whether they refer to impulses, energies, powers, and forces of nature or physiological phenomena, states, and conditions—which remain separate and distinct identities. The risk with Sallis's approach is that it is overly focused on the figures of Apollo and Dionysus and, ironically given the title of his book, does not sufficiently consider their "crossing." The philosophical background of Nietzsche's considerations on tragedy and philosophy, by contrast, strongly suggests that the "zwiespältige" entanglement of Apollo and Dionysus in a "monstrous opposition" and "open conflict" means that Apollo and Dionysus cannot in fact be dissolved into separate entities but are always already bound up with each other.

The opening sentence of *The Birth of Tragedy* takes a critical stance towards the Parmenidean assumption that difference, the world of the senses and intuition, is overcome and absorbed in the world of thought and reason. By alerting his readers in the first sentence that the continuous development of art is realised "not just through logical insight but also with the certainty of something directly apprehended," Nietzsche might be gesturing toward the need to rescue art from the Parmenidean denial of the world of sensation. Nietzsche does not negate logical insight or reason per se; rather, the latter stand on "something directly apprehended" that precedes it, much like the way in which the Apollonian is preceded by the Dionysian.

Nietzsche's reflections on philosophy in the tragic age of the Greeks confirm that "Zweiheit," including that between Apollo and Dionysus, designates neither an opposition between fixed and absolute terms nor a lack or deficit that needs to be compensated by means of an elevating unification where one principle or drive dominates the other. Rather, Zweiheit reflects the continuous struggle (Kampf) between two forces that underpins the becoming of life and art as a continuously shifting relationship of generation and transformation. When the Dionysian and the Apollonian can achieve a fruitful tension and balance, then we witness the emergence of culture, as exemplified by the Attic tragedy. Zweiheit does not refer to a splitting of Apollo and Dionysus into two separate entities. Instead, Zweiheit means Zwiespalt. It reveals an ambiguity, mix-up, and entanglement of two that cannot be dissolved into one. As such, Nietzsche's conception of Zweiheit signals the priority of relationality over identity, intuition over logical insight, plurality over unity.

III.
Kampf (Struggle) and Reconciliation (Versöhnung)

While Nietzsche rejects the notions of "unity" found in Anaximander and Parmenides, and despite his emphasis on continuous movement of struggle and conflict as the defining feature of the duality of Apollo and Dionysus, he does not give up on the idea of unity altogether in *The Birth of Tragedy*. Rather, the "reconciliation" (Versöhnung) of the Apollonian and the Dionysian marks the birth of Greek tragedy. How we are to understand this "miraculous" unity?[50] The opening sentence points towards "perpetual struggle" with short intervals of reconciliation as the distinguishing feature of the pairing of Apollo and Dionysus, suggesting that this unity is not a permanent one but subject to continuous transformation and transfiguration.

The semantic field of conflict, struggle, competition, and agon is a complex one.[51] Indeed, will to power and conflict or agon are not the same thing. Will to power refers to an entanglement of drives in perpetual struggle for and against each other. In *The Birth of Tragedy*, this relationship is exemplified by the struggle between the artistic and generative forces of nature of which the Apollonian and the Dionysian are an expression. Agon, instead, refers to a particular cultural institution in the Greek polis, which for Nietzsche underpins the advancement of Greek culture in the sixth century and, here in the opening of *The Birth of Tragedy*, the continuous development of art and the future generation of humanity. What Nietzsche admires in the cultural institution of agon is that it channels the artistic forces of nature into the generation of art without dominating or controlling them. In contrast to "modern ideas," as Nietzsche calls them in *The Birth of Tragedy*, the Greek practice of agon is not an immunitary but a communitary practice that thinks together and in a relationship Apollo and Dionysus, reason and intuition, nature and culture, rather than separating them into individual entities or identities. Because struggle and conflict in Nietzsche are not identitary or immunitary, we can say that they are transformative, creative, and oriented towards birth and creativity as opposed to preservation and protection.

Nietzsche's conception of the conflicting relationship between two in *The Birth of Tragedy* signals a shift from a thinking of identity to a thinking of relationality. Elsewhere in Nietzsche, whether we are talking about Nietzsche's conception of the will to power or the relationship between lovers, friends, and enemies, or even the relationship one entertains with oneself rendered by the well-known motto "become who you are," we always find the underlying uncanny (*ungeheuren*) and conflicting (*zwiespältigen*) pairing of Apollo and Dionysus that underpins Nietzsche's thinking about unity.

It is therefore not surprising that, after *The Birth of Tragedy*, Nietzsche returns to the term Zweiheit predominantly in the context of his reflections on relationships, including to oneself. I have argued elsewhere that Nietzsche's thinking of Zweiheit and the becoming of the self is perhaps best illustrated by his own "Attempt at Self-Criticism," prefacing *The Birth of Tragedy* and written in 1886.[52] Nietzsche's prefaces provide an example of the continuous doubling of the past reflected in a return to the past that breaks open the past and reorients it toward the future. The underlying premise of Nietzsche's project of preface writing was that the past is not yet defined, determined, and fixed, but open to "an attempt to give oneself, as it were *a posteriori*, a past in which one would like to originate in opposition to that in which one did originate."[53] Such an attempt requires adopting the perspective of Zweiheit, where the two are irreducible to each other, inscribed in the conflicting (zwiespältigen) movement of "becoming who you are."

Ecce Homo concludes the project of preface writing and offers a good example of how Nietzsche approaches the question of unity, here that of his life and thought, as well as that of his oeuvre. *Ecce Homo* reflects Nietzsche's attempt to articulate the irreducible possibilities of life and thought exemplified in his own philosophy. As such, it is a book that traces the multifaceted struggles that traverse Nietzsche's philosophical life while at the same time offering an attempt at reconciliation. In *Ecce Homo*, Nietzsche wants to recollect himself, to show the coherence of his work, and to affirm it as such. However, this self-concentration can only be expressed by a rupture and a confusion between Nietzsche and Nietzsche. To consider himself identical to himself is impossible, and he therefore rejects the idea that a philosophical work must be systematic and closed. Instead, a philosophical work should reflect a plurality of views that neither exclude nor complement each other but tell the story of the philosopher's self-experimentations and self-overcoming, fragmenting rather than unifying. As Derrida has pointed out, Nietzsche's preferred metaphor of "self-identity" is "dynamite" or "explosive material."[54] Nietzsche rejects the pretension of a proper identity, stable and folded over itself, built on the illusion of personal identity as a fixed property, which leads Derrida to speak of Nietzsche's signatures as signs of his multiple identities. Accordingly, "becoming who one is" arises neither from self-knowledge nor self-mastery—as the opening sentence of *The Birth of Tragedy* indicates, "logical insight" alone is not sufficient to grasp unity. Instead, becoming who one is is always occurring through something other than the self, something which paradoxically always remains at an irreducible distance from the self. In other words, there can be no relationship without distance.

Distance is also the key word that describes Nietzsche's conception of love. In *The Wanderer and His Shadow*, Nietzsche defines love as a relationship between two (Zweiheit) where the self is not dissolved, overcome, or sublimated in or by the other in view of constituting a higher unity.[55] On the contrary, love means "understanding and rejoicing that another lives, works, and feels in a different and opposite way to ourselves. That love may be able to bridge over the contrast (*Gegensätze*) by joy, we must not remove (*aufheben*) or deny those contrasts. Even self-love presupposes an irreconcilable (*unvermischbare*) duality (Zweiheit) (or plurality [*Vielheit*]) in one person."[56] Just as in Greek tragedy, where Apollonian *Schein* overcomes the Dionysian insight into the abyss of nature, without thereby eliminating it, love affirms the impossibility of the One.

Beyond the realm of interpersonal relationships, the continuous dissolution of unity into Zweiheit occurs in Nietzsche's thinking about psychology, morality, politics, and the state. Uncovering plurality, two, where commonly the history of philosophy saw only one, is a key feature of Nietzsche's philosophising with a hammer.[57] In his later work, Zweiheit names plurality as what resists being inscribed within the identity of the one. His critique of morality, for example, questions the commonly accepted notion of willing "something that is a unit only as a word" and the associated conception of the ego: "We are accustomed to disregard this duality (Zweiheit) and to deceive ourselves about it by means of the synthetic concept 'I,'" culminating in the idea of "freedom of the will."[58] This moral illusion of identity also translates into images of political unity, reflected, for example, in the famous exclamation of Louis XIV, "*l'État, c'est moi,*" which Nietzsche parodies as "*L'effet c'est moi*: what happens here is what happens in every well-constructed and happy commonwealth, namely, the governing class identifies itself with the successes of the commonwealth."[59] Where the ruling classes see only one, for Nietzsche the task of the philosopher is to uncover two.[60]

Nietzsche's conception of struggle and reconciliation in *The Birth of Tragedy* culminates in his philosophy of will to power, now articulated through the relationship between power and resistance: "The will to power can only be expressed through resistance; he looks for what resists him."[61] According to Nietzsche's conception of power, the relationship between ruler and ruled does not dissolve into a permanent hierarchal ordering and unity. Rather, power is relational and horizontal to the extent that the question of unity and who rules always remains open to transgression and transformation. The pairing of power and resistance, ruler and ruled, is like that of Apollo and Dionysus, where the "monstrous opposition (ungeheure Gegensatz)" and "open conflict (offnen Zwiespalt)" between the two forces generate the becoming of the work of art and the future of humanity. The priority of relationality over identity ensures that twoness is not collapsed into oneness. It prohibits the resolution of power into domination. When the Dionysian and the Apollonian are in balance, it manifests itself as a creating together. This creative balance between Dionysus and Apollo, struggle and reconciliation, turns into domination under the rule of Socratism, resulting in decline of Greek culture. Nietzsche's philosophy of duality, conflict, and relationality seeks to reverse this constellation of power, and as such provides an answer to the problem of domination that still today defines our present time.

1 Friedrich Nietzsche, *The Birth of Tragedy and Other Writings*, trans. Ronald Speirs (Cambridge University Press, 1999).

2 Friedrich Nietzsche, *Sämtliche Werke, Kritische Studienausgabe in 15 Bänden*, ed. Giorgio Colli and Mazzino Montinari (De Gruyter, 1988), KSA 1.

3 See, for example, Alain Badiou, "Who is Nietzsche?" *Pli* 11 (2011): 1–11 and Alenka Zupančič, *The Shortest Shadow: Nietzsche's Philosophy of the Two* (MIT, 2003).

4 EH, "Why I Write Such Good Books," "The Untimely Ones," 2. Friedrich Nietzsche, *The Anti-Christ, Ecce Homo, Twilight of the Idols, and Other Writings*, ed. Judith Norman and Aaron Ridley, trans. Judith Norman (Cambridge University Press, 2005).

5 Adrian Del Caro, *Grounding the Nietzsche Rhetoric of Earth* (De Gruyter, 2004), 22–23.

6 Del Caro, *Grounding*, 23.

7 John Sallis, *Crossings: Nietzsche and the Space of Tragedy* (University of Chicago Press, 1991), 16–17; Richard Schacht, *Nietzsche* (Routledge & Kegan Paul, 1985), 482.

8 BT 14.

9 Philipp Descola, *Beyond Nature and Culture* (Chicago University Press, 2014).

10 KSA 7:7[47] 7.149 and 7:7[123] 7.176.

11 Barbara Reibnitz, *Ein Kommentar zu Friedrich Nietzsches "Die Geburt der Tragödie aus dem Geiste der Musik*," (Metzler, 1992), 59ff; Immanuel Kant, *Werke. Band 7: Der Streit der Fakultäten; Anthropologie in pragmatischer Hinsicht* (De Gruyter, 2020), 177ff.

12 Reibnitz, *Kommentar*, 59.

13 Carlotta Santini, "Natur und Geschichte. Welches Paradigma für das Studium der griechischen Literatur," in *Nietzsches Naturen*, eds. Vanessa Lemm and Antonia Ulrich (De Gruyter, 2024), 125–144.

14 BT, "An Attempt at Self-Criticism," 2

15 Wolfgang Riedel, *"Homo Natura": Literarische Anthropologie um 1900* (De Gruyter, 1996).

16 For an earlier iteration of this argument in relation to Nietzsche's philosophical anthropology, see Vanessa Lemm, *Homo Natura: Friedrich Nietzsche, Philosophical Anthropology and Biopolitics* (Edinburgh University Press, 2020). The following paragraphs are drawn from chapter four with slight modifications.

17 Riedel, *"Homo Natura,"* 159–60.

18 Riedel, 206.

19 As cited by Riedel, 172.

20 As I argue in *Homo Natura*, this idea is also reflected in Nietzsche's understanding of the naturalisation of philosophy and the project to think about human nature from the perspective of the otherness of nature.

21 See also Vanessa Lemm, ed., *Nietzsche and the Becoming of Life* (Fordham University Press, 2014) and Barbara Stiegler, *Nietzsche et la biologie* (Presse universitaire de France. 2001).

22 BT 1.

23 BT 2.

24 KSA 7:7 [117].
25 KSA 7:7[117].
26 See Claus Zittel, *Selbstaufhebungsfiguren bei Nietzsche* (Königshausen & Neuman, 1995).
27 Sallis, *Crossings*, 21.
28 Claus Zittel, "Im ‚Wirbel des Seins.' Die Geburt der *Geburt der Tragödie* aus dem Geiste Friedrich Hebbels," *Nietzsche-Studien* 52 (2022): 1–38.
29 BT 1.
30 Roberto Esposito, *Immunitas: The Protection and Negation of Life* (Polity Press, 2011).
31 BT 24.
32 BT 1.
33 BT 23.
34 BT 20.
35 KSA 7:7[47] 7.149, my translation.
36 KSA 7:7[123] 7.176).
37 David Wellbery "Die Geburt der Kunst: Zur ästhetischen Affirmation," in *Ethik der Ästhetik*, eds. Hans Ulrich Gumbrecht, Dietmar Kamper, and Christoph Wulf (Akademie Verlag, 2016), 32 (my translation).
38 Plato, *Thaetetus*, 148e.
39 Wellbery, *Die Geburt der Kunst*, 29–30.
40 Wellbery, 32.
41 BT 10.
42 BT 1.
43 PTG 5. On Nietzsche and the Greeks, see Enrico Müller, *Die Griechen im Denken Nietzsches* (De Gruyter, 2005); Paul Bishop, ed., *Nietzsche and Antiquity: His Reaction and Response to the Classical Tradition* (Camden House, 2004); Helmut Heit, "Nietzsche's Genealogy of Early Greek Philosophy," in *Nietzsche as a Scholar of Antiquity*, eds. Anthony K. Jensen and Helmut Heit (Bloomsbury, 2014), 217–32.
44 Friedrich Nietzsche, *Early Greek Philosophy & Other Essays*, ed. Oscar Levy, trans. Maximilian A. Mügge (T. N. Foulis, 1911). On Nietzsche and Heraclitus, see Jackson P. Herschbell and Stephen A. Nimis, "Nietzsche and Heraclitus," *Nietzsche-Studien* 8 (1979): 17–38; Uvo Hölscher, "Nietzsche's Debt to Heraclitus," in *Classical Influences on Western Thought A.D. 1650–1870: Proceedings of an International Conference held at King's College*, ed. R. R Bolgar (Cambridge University Press, 1977), 339–48; Scarlett Marton, "Nietzsche e Hegel, Leitores de Heráclito," in *Extravagancias: Ensayos sobre la Filosofia de Nietzsche* (Discurso Editorial & Editora Barcarolla, 2009), 119–42.
45 PTG, 1.822.
46 PTG, 1.822–3.
47 For a discussion of this view, see Vanessa Lemm, *Nietzsche's Animal Philosophy: Culture, Politics and the Animality of the Human Being* (Fordham University Press, 2009), chapter six.
48 PTG 5, 1.823.
49 PTG 12, 1.849–50.

50 BT 1.

51 On Nietzsche, conflict, struggle, and agon, see Christa D. Acampora, *Contesting Nietzsche* (University of Chicago Press, 2013); Herman Siemens, "Agonal Configurations in the *Unzeitgemässe Betrachtungen*. Identity, Mimesis and the *Übertragung* of Cultures in Nietzsche's Early Thought," *Nietzsche-Studien* 30 (2001): 80–106; James Pearson and Herman Siemens, eds., *Conflict and Contest in Nietzsche's Philosophy* (Bloomsbury, 2018).

52 Lemm, *Animal Philosophy*, chapter 5.

53 Friedrich Nietzsche, *Untimely Meditations*, trans. R. J. Hollingdale (Cambridge University Press, 1997). HL 3.

54 EH, "Why I Write Such Good Books," "The Untimely Ones," 3. Jacques Derrida, *Otobiographies. L'enseignement de Nietzsche et la politique du nom propre* (Galilée, 1984); Jacques Derrida, *Spurs: Nietzsche's Styles/ Éperons. Les Styles de Nietzsche*, trans. Barbara Harlow (University of Chicago Press, 1979).

55 WS 75.

56 Friedrich Nietzsche, *Human All too Human* (University of Cambridge, 1997).

57 TI, "The Four Great Errors."

58 BGE, 19.

59 BGE, 19.

60 See also on contesting sensations and Zweiheit, KSA 10:1[73] 10.29 and on will and Zweiheit, KSA 11:38[8] 11.606.

61 KSA 12:9[151] 12.424(104).

Introduction: Nietzschean Vibe Shifts
by Paris Lettau and Vincent Lê

Andreessen, Marc. "The Techno-Optimist Manifesto." *Andreessen Horowitz*, October 16, 2023. Accessed December 13, 2024. https://a16z.com/the-techno-optimist-manifesto/.

Bronze Age Pervert. *Bronze Age Mindset: An Exhortation*. Independently published, 2018. eBook.

Kaufmann, Walter. *Nietzsche: Philosopher, Psychologist, Antichrist*. Princeton University Press, 1974.

Nietzsche, Friedrich. "The Anti-Christ: A Curse on Christianity." In *The Anti-Christ, Ecce Homo, Twilight of the Idols, and Other Writings*, edited by Aaron Ridley and Judith Norman, translated by Judith Norman, 3–67. Cambridge University Press, 2005.

1 The Death of Nietzsche
by Caitlyn Lesiuk

Barthes, Roland. "The Death of the Author." In *Image, Music, Text*, 142–48. Translated by Stephen Heath. Fontana, 1977.

Elden, Stuart. "Introduction: A Study of Productive Tensions." In *Metaphilosophy*, by Henri Lefebvre, xi–xxvii, edited by Stuart Elden. Translated by David Fernbach. Verso, 2016.

Faulkner, Joanne. *Dead Letters to Nietzsche, or the Necromantic Art of Reading Philosophy*. Ohio University Press, 2010.

Foucault, Michel. "Two Lectures." In *Power/Knowledge: Selected Interviews and Other Writings, 1972–1977*, 78–108, edited by Colin Gordon. Harvester Press, 1980.

Lampert, Laurence. *What a Philosopher Is: Becoming Nietzsche*. University of Chicago Press, 2017.

Lefebvre, Henri. *Hegel, Marx, Nietzsche or the Realm of Shadows*. Translated by David Fernbach. Verso, 2020.

Losurdo, Domenico. *Nietzsche, the Aristocratic Rebel: Intellectual Biography and Critical Balance-Sheet*. Translated by Gregor Benton. Brill, 2019.

Lukács, György. *The Destruction of Reason*. Translated by Peter Palmer. Verso, 2021.

Neuhaus, Susan. "Images of Service and Sacrifice – Tracing Narratives in Stained Glass." *Journal of Military and Veterans' Health* 26, no. 4 (October 2018): 26–31. https://doi.org/10.3316/informit.077276636624342.

Nietzsche, Friedrich. *The Birth of Tragedy*. Translated by Douglas Smith. Oxford University Press, 2000.

Nietzsche, Friedrich. *Ecce Homo*. Translated by R. J. Hollingdale. Penguin, 2004.

Prideaux, Sue. *I Am Dynamite! A Life of Nietzsche*. Faber & Faber, 2018.
Plato. "Apology." In *Plato: Complete Works*, edited by John M. Cooper, translated by G. M. A. Grube, 17–36. Hackett Publishing Company, 1997.
Ratner-Rosenhagen, Jennifer. *American Nietzsche: A History of an Icon and His Ideas*. University of Chicago Press, 2012.
Sloterdijk, Peter. *Nietzsche Apostle*. Translated by Steve Corcoran. MIT Press, 2013.
Waite, Geoffrey. *Nietzsche's Corps/e: Aesthetics, Politics, Prophecy, or, The Spectacular Technoculture of Everyday Life*. Duke University Press, 1996.

2 The Forced Choice of Post-Modernism: Alenka Zupančič's Nietzsche by Rex Butler

Baudrillard, Jean. *Fragments: Conversations with François L'Yvonnet*. Routledge, 2004.
——. *In the Shadow of the Silent Majorities*. Semiotext(e), 2007.
Deleuze, Gilles, and Félix Guattari. *A Thousand Plateaus: Capitalism and Schizophrenia*. University of Minneapolis Press, 1987.
Derrida, Jacques. "Of an Apocalyptic Tone Recently Adopted in Philosophy." *Oxford Literary Review* 6, no. 2 (1984): 3–37.
——. "Structure, Sign and Play in the Discourse of the Human Sciences." In *Writing and Difference*, 354. Routledge, 2001.
Lacan, Jacques. *Seminar XI: The Four Fundamentals of Psycho-Analysis*. Routledge, 2018.
Lyotard, Jean-François. *The Postmodern Condition: A Report on Knowledge*. University of Minnesota Press, 1984.
——. *Lessons on the Analytic of the Sublime: Kant's Critique of Judgement 23–29*. Meridian, 1994.
Popper, Karl. "Falsifiability." In *The Logic of Scientific Discovery*, 57–73. Routledge, 2002.
Weber, Max. *The Protestant Ethic and the Spirit of Capitalism*. Roxbury Publishing, 2002.
Žižek, Slavoj. *Did Somebody Say Totalitarianism? Five Interventions in the (Mis)use of a Notion*. Verso, 2001.
——. "Clinton, Trump and the Left's Dilemma." *In These Times*, 6 November 2016. https://inthesetimes.com/features/zizek_clinton_trump_lesser_evil.html.
Zupančič, Alenka. *The Shortest Shadow: Nietzsche's Philosophy of the Two*. MIT Press, 2003.

3 Dionysos in the Antipodes: Nietzsche, Norman and Jack Lindsay, Bernard Smith
by Ian McLean

Ansell-Pearson, Keith. "Nietzsche, Woman and Political Theory." In *Nietzsche, Feminism and Political Theory*, edited by Paul Patton, 1–20. Routledge, 1993.

Beilharz, Peter. *Imagining the Antipodes: Culture, Theory, and the Visual in the Work of Bernard Smith.* Cambridge University Press, 1997.

Binion, Rudolph. *Frau Lou: Nietzsche's Wayward Disciple.* Princeton University Press, 1968.

Copeland, Julie. "Bernard Smith a Reluctant Icon." *Artlink* 26, no. 4 (2006): 82–85.

Derrida, Jacques. *Spurs Nietzsche's Styles/Eperons: Les Styles de Nietzsche.* Translated by Barbara Harlow. University of Chicago Press, 1979.

Gooding-Williams, Robert. *Zarathustra's Dionysian Modernism.* Stanford University Press, 2001.

Graybeal, Jean. *Language and "the Feminine" in Nietzsche and Heidegger.* Indiana University Press, 1990.

Lindsay, Jack. "Foreword." *Vision: A Literary Quarterly* no. 1 (May 1923): 2–3.

Lindsay, Jack. *The Anatomy of Spirit: An Inquiry into the Origins of Religious Emotion.* Methuen, 1937.

——. *Dionysos Nietzsche Contra Nietzsche: An Essay in Lyrical Philosophy.* Fanfrolico Press, 1928.

——. *The Fullness of Life: Autobiography of an Idea.* Edited by Anne Cranny-Francis. Fanfrolico Press, c. 1970.

——. *Life Rarely Tells.* The Bodley Head, 1958.

——. *A Short History of Culture.* Victor Gollancz, 1939.

——. "Zarathustra in Queensland." *Meanjin* 7, no. 4 (1948): 211–25.

Lindsay, Norman. *Creative Effort: An Essay in Affirmation.* Art in Australia, 1920.

——. *My Mask.* Angus and Robertson, 1970.

McLean, Ian. "Bernard Smith's Blind Spot: Aboriginal and Australian Art." In *The Legacies of Bernard Smith: Essays on Australian Art, History and Cultural Politics*, edited by Jaynie Anderson, Christopher R. Marshall, and Andrew Yip, 338–50. Power Publications and Art Gallery of NSW, 2016.

——. *Double Nation: A History of Australian Art.* Reaktion Books, 2023.

Nietzsche, Friedrich. *Beyond Good and Evil.* Translated by Judith Norman. Cambridge University Press, 2002.

——. *The Birth of Tragedy or Hellenism and Pessimism.* Translated by Wm. A. Haussmann. George Allen & Unwin, 1923.

——. *Ecce Homo.* Translated by Anthony M. Ludovici. Macmillan, 1911.

——. "Ecce Homo: How to Become What You Are." In *The Anti-Christ, Ecce Homo, Twilight of the Idols, and Other Writings,* edited by Aaron Ridley and Judith Norman, 69–152. Cambridge University Press, 2005.

——. *The Gay Science.* Translated by Josefine Nauckhoff. Cambridge University Press, 2001.

——. "On the Genealogy of Morals." Translated by Walter Kaufmann and R. J. Hollingdale. In *On the Genealogy of Morals; Ecce Homo,* edited by Walter Kaufmann, 15–200. Vintage Books, 1967.

——. "On the Uses and Disadvantages of History for Life." Translated by R. J. Hollingdale. In *Untimely Meditations,* 57–123. Cambridge University Press, 1997.

——. *Thus Spoke Zarathustra: A Book for All and None.* Translated by Alexander Tille. The Macmillan Company, 1896.

——. *Thus Spoke Zarathustra: A Book for All and None.* Translated by Adrian Del Caro. Edited by Adrian Del Caro and Robert Pippin. Cambridge University Press, 2006.

——. *The Will to Power.* Translated by Walter Kaufmann and R. J. Hollingdale. Vintage Books, 1968.

——. *Unpublished Fragments (Spring 1885–Spring 1886).* Edited by Duncan Large and Alan D. Schrift. Translated by Adrian Del Caro. *The Complete Works of Friedrich Nietzsche*, volume 16. Stanford University Press, 2020.

Palmer, Sheridan. *Hegel's Owl: The Life of Bernard Smith.* Power Publications, 2016.

Patton, Paul, ed. *Nietzsche, Feminism and Political Theory.* Routledge, 1993.

Salomé, Lou. *Nietzsche.* Translated by Siegfried Mandel. Urbana and University of Illinois Press, 2001.

Smith, Bernard. "The Antipodean Manifesto." In *The Death of the Artist as Hero: Essays in History and Culture,* 194–97. Oxford University Press, 1988.

——. "Creators and Catalysts: The Modernisation of Australian Indigenous Art." *Australian Cultural History* 26 (2006): 11–25.

——. "Introduction: A Bibliographic Memoir." In *The Writings of Bernard Smith, Bibliography 1938–1998,* edited by John Spencer and Peter Wright, 3–14. Power Publications, 2000.

——. "Is There a Radical Tradition in Australian Art?" In *The Death of the Artist as Hero: Essays in History and Culture,* 230–40. Oxford University Press, 1988.

——. "Jack Lindsay." In *The Death of the Artist as Hero: Essays in History and Culture,* 103–16. Oxford University Press, 1988.

——. "Jack Lindsay's Marxism." In *The Death of the Artist as Hero: Essays in History and Culture,* 117–29. Oxford University Press, 1988.

——. *Modernism's History: A Study of Twentieth-Century Art and Ideas.* UNSW Press, 1998.

——. "Notes on Abstract Art." In *The Death of the Artist as Hero: Essays in History and Culture,* 181–93. Oxford University Press, 1988.

——. "Notes on Elitism and the Arts." In *The Death of the Artist as Hero: Essays in History and Culture*, 3–7. Oxford University Press, 1988.

——. "On Cultural Convergence." In *The Death of the Artist as Hero: Essays in History and Culture*, 289–302. Oxford University Press, 1988.

——. *Place, Taste and Tradition: A Study of Australian Art since 1788.* 2nd ed. Oxford University Press, 1979.

——. *The Spectre of Truganini: 1980 Boyer Lectures.* Australian Broadcasting Commission, 1980.

——. "The Truth About the Antipodeans." In *The Death of the Artist as Hero: Essays in History and Culture*, 199–213. Oxford University Press, 1988.

Smith, Bernard, with Terry Smith. *Australian Painting 1788–1990.* Oxford University Press, 1991.

4 Taking Flight from Oneself: Nietzsche on the Poets, Baudelaire, and the Little Parisian Decadents
by Keith Ansell-Pearson

Baudelaire, Charles. *The Flowers of Evil.* Translated by James McGowan. Oxford University Press, 1993.

——. *Selected Writings on Art and Literature.* Translated by P. E. Charvet. Penguin, 2006.

——. *My Heart Laid Bare & Other Texts.* Translated with an introduction by Rainer J. Hanshe. Contra Mundum Press, 2020.

——. *Late Fragments.* Translated with an introduction by Richard Sieburth. Yale University Press, 2022.

Benjamin, Walter. "Hashish in Marseilles." In *Reflections: Essays, Aphorisms, Autobiographical Writings*, 137–46. Harcourt Brace Jovanovich, 1978.

——. *The Writer of Modern Life: Essays on Charles Baudelaire.* Edited by Michael W. Jennings. Harvard University Press, 2006.

Bernheimer, Charles. *Decadent Subjects: The Idea of Decadence in Art, Literature, Philosophy, and Culture of the Fin de Siècle in Europe.* Edited by T. Jefferson Kline and Naomi Schor. Johns Hopkins University Press, 2002.

Bersani, Leo. *Baudelaire and Freud.* University of California Press, 1977.

Bertram, Ernst. *Studien zu Adalbert Stifters Novellentechnik.* Fr. Wilh. Ruhfus, 1907.

——. *Nietzsche: Attempt at a Mythology.* Translated by Robert E. Norton. University of Illinois Press, 2009. First published 1918.

Blackhall, Eric A. *Adalbert Stifter.* Cambridge University Press, 1948.

Bourget, Paul. *Essais de psychologie contemporaine.* Gallimard, 1993. First published 1883.

——. "The Example of Baudelaire." Translated by Nancy O'Connor, *New England Review* 30, no. 2 (2009): 90–104.

Bruford, W. H. *The German Tradition of Self-Cultivation: "Bildung" from Humboldt to Thomas Mann*. Cambridge University Press, 1975.

Chambers, Ross. *An Atmospherics of the City: Baudelaire and the Poetics of Noise*. Fordham University Press, 2015.

Calasso, Roberto. *La Folie Baudelaire*. Translated by Alistair McEwen. Penguin, 2012.

Conway, Daniel W. *Nietzsche's Dangerous Game: Philosophy in the Twilight of the Idols*. Cambridge University Press, 1997.

De Quincey, Thomas. *Confessions of an English Opium Eater*. Penguin, 1971 (original work published 1821).

Eliot, T. S. "Baudelaire." In *Selected Prose of T. S. Eliot*, edited with an introduction by Frank Kermode, 231–37. Faber & Faber, 1975.

Emerson, Ralph Waldo. *The Essential Writings of Ralph Waldo Emerson*. Edited by Brooks Atkinson. Modern Library, 2000.

——. *The Conduct of Life*. Harvard University Press, 2003.

Gogröf-Voorhees, Andrea. *Defining Modernism: Baudelaire and Nietzsche on Romanticism, Modernity, Decadence, and Wagner*. Peter Lang, 2004.

Gump, Margaret. *Adalbert Stifter*. Twayne Publishers, 1974.

Harvey, Ryan, and Aaron Ridley. *Nietzsche's "The Case of Wagner" and "Nietzsche contra Wagner."* Edinburgh University Press, 2022.

Huddleston, Andrew. *Nietzsche on the Decadence and Flourishing of Culture*. Oxford University Press, 2019.

Isherwood, Christopher. *Exhumations*. Penguin, 1969.

James, Henry. *The Critical Muse: Selected Literary Criticism*. Edited with an introduction by Roger Gard. Penguin, 1987.

Middleton, Christopher. *Selected Letters of Friedrich Nietzsche*. Hackett, 1996.

Montinari, Mazzino. *Reading Nietzsche*. Translated by Greg Whitlock. University of Illinois Press, 2003.

Nietzsche, Friedrich. *Beyond Good and Evil*. Translated by Adrian del Caro. Stanford University Press, 2014.

——. *The Birth of Tragedy*. Translated by Ronald Speirs. Cambridge University Press, 1999.

——. *Ecce Homo*. Translated by Duncan Large. Oxford University Press, 2007.

——. *The Gay Science*. Translated by Walter Kaufmann. Random House, 1974.

——. *Human, All Too Human*. Translated by Gary Handwerk. Stanford University Press, 1995.

——. *Mixed Opinions and Maxims & The Wanderer and His Shadow*. Translated by Gary Handwerk. Stanford University Press, 2013.

——. *Sämtliche Werke: Kritische Studienausgabe*. De Gruyter, 1988.

——. *Unfashionable Observations: Schopenhauer as Educator*. Translated by Richard T. Gray. Stanford University Press, 1995.

O'Brown, Norman. *Life Against Death: The Psychoanalytical Meaning of History*. Sphere Books, 1968 (original work published 1959).

Pearson, Roger. *The Beauty of Baudelaire: The Poet as Alternative Lawgiver*. Oxford University Press, 2021.
Pestalozzi, Karl. "Nietzsche's Baudelaire-Rezeption." *Nietzsche-Studien* 7 (1978): 158–78.
Santayana, George. *Selected Critical Writings of George Santayana*. Volume One. Edited by Norman Henfrey. Cambridge University Press, 1968.
Stifter, Adalbert. *Bunte Steine*. Reclam, 1994.
——. *Nachsommer*. Reclam, 2005.
——. *Indian Summer*. Translated by Wendell Frye. Bern: Peter Lang, 2009.
——. *Motley Stones*. Translated by Isabel Fargo Cole. New York Review Books, 2021.
Swales, Martin, and Erika Swales. *Adalbert Stifter: A Critical Study*. Cambridge University Press, 1984.
Swart, Koenraad W. *The Sense of Decadence in Nineteenth-Century France*. Martinus Nijhoff, 1964.
Valéry, Paul. *Leonardo, Poe, Mallarmé*. Translated by Malcolm Cowley and James R. Lawler. Routledge & Kegan Paul, 1972.

5 We Have Ways of Making You Talk:
Parsing Nietzsche's Philology
by Jason Barker and Justin Clemens

Arendt, Hannah. *The Human Condition*. University of Chicago Press, 1958.
Axelos, Kostas. *The Game of the World*. Translated by Justin Clemens and Hellmut Monz. Edinburgh University Press, 2023.
Badiou, Alain. "Who Is Nietzsche?" *Pli* 11 (2001): 2.
Bluhm, Heinz. "Nietzsche's Final View of Luther and the Reformation." *PMLA* 71, no. 1 (1956): 75.
Chaitin, Gregory J. "Algorithmic Information Theory." *IBM Journal of Research and Development* 4 (1977): 350–59.
During, Elie. "Deleuze and Nietzsche: On Frivolous Propositions and Related Matters." *Pli* 11 (2001): 71.
Hamacher, Werner, and Catharine Diehl. "95 Theses on Philology." *Diacritics* 39, no. 1 (2009): 40–41.
Kant, Immanuel. *Critique of the Power of Judgment*. Edited and translated by Paul Guyer and Eric Matthews. Cambridge University Press, 2013.
Lampert, Laurence. *Nietzsche and Modern Times: A Study of Bacon, Descartes, and Nietzsche*. Yale University Press, 1993.
Milner, Jean-Claude, Ann Banfield, and Daniel Heller-Roazen. "Interview with Jean-Claude Milner." *S: Journal of the Circle for Lacanian Ideology Critique* 3 (2010): 4.
Nietzsche, Friedrich. *Daybreak: Thoughts on the Prejudices of Morality*. Edited by Maudemarie Clark and Brian Leiter, translated by R. J. Hollingdale. Cambridge University Press, 1997.

——. "Attempt at a Self-Criticism." In *The Birth of Tragedy*, translated by Douglas Smith, 12–13. Oxford University Press, 2000.
——. *Homer and Classical Philology*. In *The Complete Works of Friedrich Nietzsche*, vol. 3, edited by Oscar Levy and translated by J. M. Kennedy. Edinburgh and T. N. Foulis, 1910.
——. *On the Future of Our Educational Institutions*. Translated by J. M. Kennedy. T. N. Foulis, 1910.
——. *Selected Letters of Friedrich Nietzsche*. Edited and translated by Christopher Middleton. Hackett, 1996.
——. *Unfashionable Observations*. Translated by Richard T. Gray. Stanford University Press, 1995.
——. *Unpublished Fragments (Spring 1885–Spring 1886)*. Edited by Duncan Large and Alan D. Schrift. Translated by Adrian Del Caro. *The Complete Works of Friedrich Nietzsche*, volume 16. Stanford University Press, 2020.
——. *Writings from the Late Notebooks*. Edited by Rüdiger Bittner and translated by Kate Sturge. Cambridge University Press, 2003.
Porter, James I. "'Don't Quote Me on That!': Wilamowitz Contra Nietzsche in 1872 and 1873." *Journal of Nietzsche Studies* 42, no. 1 (2011): 73–99.
——. *Nietzsche and the Philology of the Future*. Stanford University Press, 2000.
Rohde, Erwin. *Psyche: The Cult of Souls and Belief in Immortality Among the Greeks*. Translated by W. B. Hillis. Kegan Paul, Trench, Trubner & Co., 1925.
Tyndall, John. *Fragments of Science: A Series of Detached Essays, Addresses, and Reviews*, vol. 2. Longmans, Green and Co., 1879.
Zupančič, Alenka. *The Shortest Shadow: Nietzsche's Philosophy of the Two*. MIT Press, 2003.

6 Nietzsche's *The Birth of Tragedy*: A Philosophy of Duality, Conflict, and Relationality by Vanessa Lemm

Acampora, Christa Davis. *Contesting Nietzsche*. University of Chicago Press, 2013.
Badiou, Alain. "Who Is Nietzsche?" *Pli* 11 (2001): 1–11.
Bishop, Paul, ed. *Nietzsche and Antiquity*. Camden House, 2004.
Del Caro, Adrian. *Grounding the Nietzsche Rhetoric of Earth*. De Gruyter, 2004.
Derrida, Jacques. *Otobiographies. L'enseignement de Nietzsche et la politique du nom propre*. Galilée, 1984.
——. *Spurs: Nietzsche's Styles / Éperons. Les Styles de Nietzsche*. Translated by Barbara Harlow. University of Chicago Press, 1979.
Descola, Philippe. *Beyond Nature and Culture*. University of Chicago Press, 2014.

Esposito, Roberto. *Immunitas: The Protection and Negation of Life*. Polity Press, 2011.

Heit, Helmut. "Nietzsche's Genealogy of Early Greek Philosophy." In *Nietzsche as a Scholar of Antiquity*, edited by Anthony K. Jensen and Helmut Heit, 217–32. Bloomsbury, 2014.

Herschbell, Jackson P., and Stephen A. Nimis. "Nietzsche and Heraclitus." *Nietzsche-Studien* 8, no. 1 (1979): 17–38.

Hölscher, Uvo. "Nietzsche's Debt to Heraclitus." In *Classical Influences on Western Thought A. D. 1650–1870: Proceedings of an International Conference held at King's College*, edited by R. R. Bolgar, 339–48. Cambridge University Press, 1977.

Kant, Immanuel. *Werke. Band 7: Der Streit der Fakultäten; Anthropologie in pragmatischer Hinsicht*. De Gruyter, 2020.

Lemm, Vanessa. *Nietzsche's Animal Philosophy: Culture, Politics, and the Animality of the Human Being*. Fordham University Press, 2009.

——. ed. *Nietzsche and the Becoming of Life*. Fordham University Press, 2020.

——. *Homo Natura: Nietzsche, Philosophical Anthropology, and Biopolitics*. Edinburgh University Press, 2020.

Marton, Scarlett. "Nietzsche e Hegel, leitores de Heráclito." In *Extravagancias: Ensayos Sobre La Filosofia De Nietzsche*, 119–42. Discurso Editorial & Editora Barcarolla, 2009.

Müller, Enrico. *Die Griechen im Denken Nietzsches*. De Gruyter, 2005.

Nietzsche, Friedrich. *Early Greek Philosophy & Other Essays*. Translated by Maximilian A. Mügge, edited by Oscar Levy. T. N. Foulis, 1911.

——. *Sämtliche Werke. Kritische Studienausgabe in 15 Bänden*. Edited by Giorgio Colli and Mazzino Montinari. De Gruyter, 1988.

——. *The Birth of Tragedy and Other Writings*. Translated by Ronald Speirs. Cambridge University Press, 1999.

——. *The Anti-Christ, Ecce Homo, Twilight of the Idols, and Other Writings*. Translated by Judith Norman, edited by Judith Norman and Aaron Ridley. Cambridge University Press, 2005.

——. *Human, All Too Human*. Cambridge University Press, 1997.

——. *Untimely Meditations*. Translated by R. J. Hollingdale. Cambridge University Press, 1997.

Pearson, James, and Herman Siemens, eds. *Conflict and Contest in Nietzsche's Philosophy*. Bloomsbury, 2018.

Reibnitz, Barbara von. *Ein Kommentar zu Friedrich Nietzsches "Die Geburt der Tragödie aus dem Geiste der Musik."* Metzler, 1992.

Riedel, Wolfgang. *„Homo Natura": Literarische Anthropologie um 1900*. De Gruyter, 1996.

Sallis, John. *Crossings*. University of Chicago Press, 1991.

Santini, Carlotta. "Natur und Geschichte. Welches Paradigma für das Studium der griechischen Literatur." In *Nietzsches Naturen*, edited by Vanessa Lemm and Antonia Ulrich, 125–44. De Gruyter, 2024.

Schacht, Richard. *Nietzsche*. Routledge & Kegan Paul, 1985.

Siemens, Herman. "Agonal Configurations in the Unzeitgemässe Betrachtungen. Identity, Mimesis, and the Übertragung of Cultures in Nietzsche's Early Thought." *Nietzsche-Studien* 30 (2001): 80–106.

Stiegler, Barbara. *Nietzsche et la biologie.* Presses universitaires de France, 2001.

Wellbery, David. "Die Geburt der Kunst: Zur ästhetischen Affirmation." In *Ethik der Ästhetik,* edited by Hans Ulrich Gumbrecht, Dietmar Kamper, and Christoph Wulf, 23–36. Akademie Verlag, 2016.

Zittel, Claus. *Selbstaufhebungsfiguren bei Nietzsche.* Königshausen & Neumann, 1995.

——. "Im 'Wirbel des Seins.' Die Geburt der Geburt der Tragödie aus dem Geiste Friedrich Hebbels." *Nietzsche-Studien* 52 (2022): 1–38.

Zupančič, Alenka. *The Shortest Shadow: Nietzsche's Philosophy of the Two.* MIT Press, 2003.

Keith Ansell-Pearson is Emeritus Professor of Philosophy at the University of Warwick. His book, *Nietzsche's Earthbound Wisdom. The Philosopher, the Poet, and the Sage* is published in 2025 by University of Chicago Press.

Jason Barker is Professor of Global Communication at Kyung Hee University.

Rex Butler teaches Art History in the Faculty of Art, Design and Architecture at Monash University. He has recently edited *On the Act of Looking: On Joshua Oppenheimer's Diptych* with David Denny. He is currently working on a monograph on the American critic and art historian Rosalind Krauss.

Justin Clemens FAHA works at the intersection of literary studies, psychoanalysis, and contemporary European philosophy. Among his scholarly publications are *Barron Field in New South Wales* (Melbourne UP 2023), co-authored with Thomas H. Ford. He is Associate Professor in the School of Culture and Communication at the University of Melbourne.

Vincent Lê is a philosopher, PhD graduate from Monash University, and former researcher in The Terraforming think tank. As a tutor and lecturer in philosophy, art theory, and political theory, he has haunted the classrooms of the University of Melbourne, Monash University, Deakin University, and the Melbourne School of Continental Philosophy. More of his ravings can be found via *Urbanomic*, *Hypatia, Cosmos and History*, and *Art and Australia*, among other publications. He is a founding editor of the art history and cultural theory publishing house Index Press. His research focuses on the philosophy of intelligence at the intersection of economics, artificial intelligence, and the post-Kantian transcendental tradition. He also writes at vincentl3.substack.com.

Vanessa Lemm is Professor of Political Philosophy and Deputy Vice-Chancellor & Provost at the University of Greenwich, London, UK. She is an Honorary Professorial Fellow at the Faculty of Arts at the University of Melbourne, Australia. She has published widely on the philosophy of Friedrich Nietzsche, contemporary political thought, biopolitics, posthumanism, and animal and plant studies. She is the author of *Nietzsche's Animal Philosophy: Culture, Politics and the Animality of the Human Being* (Fordham University Press, 2009), *Nietzsche y el pensamiento político contemporáneo* (Fondo de Cultura Economica, 2013), and *Homo Natura: Nietzsche, Philosophical Anthropology and Biopolitics* (EUP, 2020). She recently published with Miguel Vatter the edited volume *The Viral Politics of Covid-19: Nature, Home and Planetary Health* (Palgrave 2022) and *Nietzsche's Natures* (De Gruyter 2024) with Antonia Ulrich. She is the Editor of *Nietzsche-Studien* and associated book series at De Gruyter. Her work has been translated into six languages.

Caitlyn Lesiuk is the convenor of the Melbourne School of Continental Philosophy and a PhD candidate at Deakin University. Recently she has written for *The Oxford Handbook of Modern French Philosophy* and *Angelaki*.

Paris Lettau is an art historian and lawyer based in Melbourne, Australia. He is a founding editor of several Australian-based publications, including *Memo Review* and *Index Journal*, and the publishing house Index Press. He is Editor-In-Chief of *Memo* magazine. His writing has appeared in various books and journals, including *Ends of Painting: Art in the 1960s and 1970s* (Power Publications, 2023), *Curating Lively Objects: Exhibitions Beyond Disciplines* (Routledge, 2021), *The Field Revisited* (NGV, 2018), *Art Monthly Australia*, *Artlink*, and *Broadsheet*.

Ian McLean is an Honorary Professorial Fellow and the inaugural Hugh Ramsay Chair of Australian Art History at the University of Melbourne.